JAGUAR

Foulis

©Piagraph Limited and The Haynes Publishing Group 1975
First published by Ballantine Books Inc., of New York in 1971 in paperback
This hard cover edition was made in Great Britain for
The Haynes Publishing Group
Sparkford, Yeovil, Somerset BA22 7JJ
First published in hard covers September 1975
Reprinted June 1976

ISBN 0 85429 199 7

Contents

Photographs and illustrations for this book have been selected from the following archives : Montagu Motor Museum, L Klementaski, Ronald Barker, Alan B Cross, *Autocar, Motorcycle, Old Motor Magazine*

'Something a little bit different'

I am grateful to Lord Montagu for giving me the opportunity of writing a short foreword to his new Jaguar book.

At Jaguar we have always tried to produce motor-cars that are aesthetically appealing, yet cannot be mistaken for any other marque— nor, indeed, be anything other than 'British'. Although we achieved this from the outset, it took something more for us to win acceptance with the sporting motorists of America. I think there is no doubt that our competition activities finally turned the key for us in the United States— especially our efforts at Le Mans, where we nearly always had stiff opposition from America. I remember our first exploratory trip in 1950 to see how the XK 120 roadster would perform as a British contender. At the same event Briggs Cunningham led America's postwar assault with a pair of Cadillacs; and they beat us! The Cadillacs were 10th and 11th and the Jaguars 12th and 15th after one of them had been in 3rd place for most of the race. Not an auspicious start, and I certainly did not visualize five Jaguar victories before the decade was over. Briggs' own Cunninghams always did well, and were a great credit to him; but his motto may have been: 'If you can't beat them, join them'— for when he stopped building his own cars he raced a team of D-type Jaguars himself—and with great success.

Although we no longer build sports-racing cars, we are still using our competition experience—together with the latest technology—to produce our special kind of motoring.

As I write this, I find it difficult to realize that it is nearly fifty years since we made our first motorcycle side-car—a side-car that was 'different'. I like to think that we are still producing something a little bit 'different', and that, as Lord Montagu believes, a Jaguar will always be considered 'worth writing home about'.

Sir William Lyons

'A SPECIAL KIND OF MOTORING'

All cars worthy of their salt have some mystique, but few can rival that of the Jaguar. Lacking the Bugatti's complexity, the all-round racing successes of the Ferrari, or the sheer magnificence of Rolls-Royce, Hispano-Suiza and Duesenberg, it has made the grade on inspired production engineering. There are faster cars: there are more opulent cars: there are models with superior handling characteristics — but no other factory has ever offered quite as much quality for so modest an initial outlay, whether one thinks in terms of the £385 asked for the first $2\frac{1}{2}$-litre SS Jaguar in 1936, or the £2,890 one pays for a 4.2-litre XJ6 in 1971.

The great days of the Big Cat at Le Mans are over, and as long ago as 1962 Ferrari surpassed Jaguar's record of five victories, but the marque goes marching on. The cars are still competitive even if the twin-camshaft 6-cylinder engines under their bonnets are now a quarter of a century old in conception. Look at Jaguar how you will, here is a success story. In terms of cold cash, an investor who purchased one hundred ordinary shares at £1.20 in 1952 had built up his holding in a mere nine years to nine hundred ordinaries worth £3.87 each. If one thinks in terms of numbers, 2,500 cars were delivered in 1936: in 1969 the corresponding figure was 28,391. During this period a

Prewar evolution of the Lyons Line. Right to left, 1934 SS I saloon, 1936/9 SS 100, 1936 SS Jaguar $2\frac{1}{2}$-litre

small producer of semi-sports machines and sidecars has grown into a vital component of British Leyland, Britain's largest automotive group. If internal rationalisation has split up the old Jaguar empire, it should be remembered that Sir William Lyons' contributions to BLMC included Daimler (cars and buses), Guy (commercial vehicles), and Coventry-Climax and Meadows (engines).

Jaguar share with MG and Austin the distinction of spearheading Britain's dollar export drive in the 1940s, and to this day they are the nation's largest exporters of specialist cars. Their percentage, at around fifty per cent, is still the country's best. When it comes to individual models, a ninety per cent export quota is remarkable for the newest of sports cars, yet it still applies to Jaguar's E-type at the ripe old age of ten. Alvis, Armstrong Siddeley, Lagonda, Lea-Francis and Riley have gone; Bentley, Daimler and Sunbeam are names kept alive by a mixture of sentiment and badge-engineering. Jaguar may have chosen to join the Big Battalions rather than to go on beating them, but despite this they have lost none of their individuality.

Viewed by the standards of the 1930s, the 1971 Jaguars are mass-produced: indeed, they are turned out in quantities comparable with Standards or Vauxhalls of the last pre-war decade. But even now every Jaguar is somebody's Jaguar. The last time anyone bothered to calculate the number of permutations available in the range, the score came out at 189,024. In other words, the factory could work flat out for six years without producing two identical vehicles. Since the recent rationalisation, the total has been drastically reduced, but the point remains valid.

What impresses still more is the

'The racing car of today is the touring-car of tomorrow.' 1956 D-type with 1967 E-type

sparked off the firm's final effort, the Model-810 Cord of 1936. 'Old Coffin Nose' may have aroused more excitement than any SS or Jaguar in her day, but she lasted a mere two seasons before following her sponsors into limbo.

Consider, by contrast, the Jaguar record. Perhaps few people took the original low-slung SS I coupé, with its Standard mechanical elements and its hint of Cord, too seriously in the gloomy autumn in 1931, but it sold for four seasons, and there was no mistaking the excitement which heralded the first 2½-litre Jaguar at Olympia in 1935. Two years later came the 3½-litre SS 100 two-seater, offering an untemperamental 'ton' for £445, and at the first post-war Earls Court Show in 1948 other novelties, such as the first of Alec Issigonis's Morris Minors and the full-width Phase III Hillman Minx paled into insignificance beside the solitary bronze XK 120 on the Jaguar stand. Less than twenty-four months later William Lyons scooped the pool again with the Mk VII, a six-seater saloon which combined American ideas of spaciousness with European concepts of handling. 1955 saw the compact unitary-construction 2.4-litre, yet another twin-cam closed car which would top the 100 mark and return better than 20mpg in regular use. Hot on its heels came the amazing 3.4-litre (1957), the E-type sports car at Geneva in 1961, and the Mk X in London the following autumn.

Seven years of steady competition at Le Mans established the disc brake, and rising dollar sales helped to make Jaguar one of the pioneers of automatic transmission in Europe. Even when preoccupation with touring types and a new trend in sports-car racing drove Jaguar off the circuits for good, Sir William Lyons could still pull something out of the hat. Dark hints followed the merger with the British Motor Corporation in 1966, and the formation of

firm's record of 'show-stoppers'. Skilled production engineering is backed by high quality and by the master touch of the stylist. The motor industry has bred many a 'one-speech Hamilton'. Riley's high point was the Nine of 1926, and this theme survived for thirty years on the strength of such developments as the 1935 1½-litre and the famous 2-litre Big Four of 1937. Marc Birkigt's reputation was made on Hispano-Suiza's pre-1914 Alfonso series, and consolidated in 1919 by the superb 6.6-litre H6. Even America's greatest purveyors of automobile glamour, the Auburn-Cord group, cannot match Sir William Lyons' long succession of hits. Having set the Auburn on its feet with a facelift in 1925, they scored a formidable double in 1929 with the Model-J Duesenberg and the L29 Cord. But thereafter there was an effective pause until the advent of the 1932 Auburn Twelve, and then only a fevered gathering-up of skirts

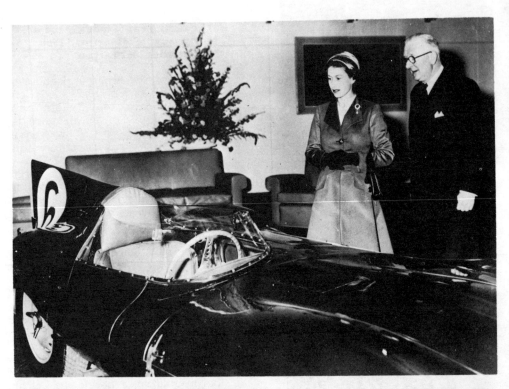

the British Leyland Group early in 1968. Unkind journalists slammed out at Jaguar's badge-engineered Daimlers and the increasingly executive image of the two marques. But the star of the 1969 model year was the safety-engineered XJ6. The Big Cat was banished from its prow, but Jaguar enthusiasts suddenly found themselves back in the Stafford Cripps era. A good twelve months after the XJ's introduction, even cash on the nail would not buy a new one.

How does Sir William Lyons do it? By long runs and brilliant production engineering, which save the customer much of the burden of rising costs. The first 2.4-litre Jaguar of 1956 retailed at £1,344: the last of the line cost only £21 more at the end of 1967. These figures alone show the advantages of a twelve-year run involving some 200,000 units. Some of the Lyons philosophy was evident in his Wakefield Gold Medal Lecture delivered in May 1969, in which he observed of his chosen sphere: 'Into this select group, we injected the Jaguar models – different in design and appearance and with a good performance, but produced in relatively large volumes to make the price realistic. I believe that, in those far-off days, we started a whole new approach to specialist cars, and one which is now expanding rapidly.'

Jaguar, in fact, had bred as well as massacred. Any specialist marque, from French exotics like the later Lago-Talbots to Euro-Americans from Railton to Gordon-Keeble, had one target to beat – Jaguar. And Jaguar, like Annie Oakley, could be confident that 'anything you can do, I can do better'. Some challengers have disappeared; some have become badge-engineered travesties of their forebears; some have

opted for safer ground. But on the other side of the coin we can see the spread of the 'personal car' in America. The late Bill Rankin, for many years Jaguar's Public Relations Officer, told me once that 'to Americans a sports car is invariably an imported car', but nevertheless the influence of the XK series and the E-type can be detected in the best-selling Ford Mustang and its imitators, Chevrolet's Camaro and Mercury's Cougar. As driver's cars they are light-years away from anything made in a British factory, but they have reintroduced a Jaguar type of 'personalisation' to the American customer, and are as much a potential competitor to the old-school specialist makers as are the new fifteen-ton trucks of the Big Battalions to the traditional hand-built type of vehicle still produced for heavy haulage on both sides of the Atlantic.

In fact Jaguar remain *hors concours.* Mercedes-Benz may outsell them, but the German firm's pre-eminence stems from its cheap and profitable diesel-engined models. Neither Ferrari nor Maserati has yet produced one-twentieth of Jaguar's output in a single year, and outside Italy owners will find service facilities extremely limited. The French *grand'routier* industry is dead, and Japan has yet to make much impact in the over-2-litre class. The American specialists are a motley crew, made up of replicas (Excalibur, Ruger, Stutz) and the remnants of Sherwood Egbert's gallant but abortive Studebaker Avanti venture. A mere 200 cars came from this sector of the industry in 1968 and one need not expect 1971's figure to be much higher.

British Leyland or no British Leyland, the story of Jaguar remains a success story, and one that is peculiarly British, from humble beginnings with Zeppelin-shaped aluminium sidecars in Blackpool to the present complex in Coventry. 'A Special Kind of Motoring' has remained special, because its creators have not only adapted themselves to the need of the moment, but have anticipated future needs.

13

SIDECARS AND SPORTY COACHWORK

In 1922 the British motorcycling press carried a description of a new line in sidecars, Zeppelin-shaped and panelled in polished aluminium. Its creators were two young Lancastrians living in Blackpool, William Lyons and William Walmsley.

This may seem an unlikely beginning for a partnership destined to evolve into the world's most famous and successful producers of specialist cars. Yet many a British factory (Hillman, Humber, Morris, Rover) cut its teeth on the bicycle, and abroad we encounter such odd products as the pepper-mills of Peugeot and Pierce-Arrow's birdcages. The solo motorcyclist, after all, progresses to the combination, thence

Making them by hand: a batch of Austin Seven Swallow two-seaters and saloons at Foleshill, 1929

to the small sports car, and finally to the executive-type saloon. So did Lyons and Walmsley. But in 1920, when the latter assembled his prototype in his parents' garage, the sidecar as a concept was only eighteen years old, having supplanted such barbarities as the trailer (unsociable and perilous on corners) and the forecarriage (prone to road dust and accidents alike). Further, it had only recently emerged from the primitive stage: coachbuilt bodies were introduced as late as 1910, by F W Mead of Birmingham, and even in 1920 the old wickerwork type was not yet defunct. What is more, coachbuilt sidecars were heavy, 'aunty' and suggestive of invalid carriages.

Walmsley's streamlined Swallow was a far more attractive proposition: the wheel was shod with a polished aluminium disc to match the body, and even when the hood was up the appearance was little-marred, though the passenger paid for this elegance by a complete absence of vision in any direction. Inevitably this one-off attracted the attention of local motorcyclists, and when the Walmsleys moved from Stockport to Blackpool in 1920 young William was brought into contact with the twenty-year-old son of a piano dealer, William Lyons.

William Lyons had no desire to enter the piano business, but he figured that there was a future in these handsome Swallow 'chairs' if they could be made at the rate of ten a week. He had, however, to wait until he attained his majority, but the moment he was of age he and Walmsley floated the Swallow Sidecar Company, with a capital of £1,000 guaranteed by their respective parents. This was, incidentally, the first and last occasion on which Lyons was to rely on outside finance.

Inevitably operations were on a modest scale. If the venture had already outgrown the confines of Walmsley's garage, Swallow's first

15

A competition model track sidecar. The passenger lay on his stomach, often for as much as 200 miles

factory, in Bloomfield Road Blackpool, employed a staff of only twelve. Nonetheless, Lyons was already running true to later form as a style leader. 1923 saw the firm's debut at a London motorcycle show, but more significant was the fact that four manufacturers, among them Brough Superior and Coventry Eagle, displayed Swallow 'chairs' on their own stands: George Brough, indeed, adopted the marque as his standard sidecar for four seasons, Brough-Swallow outfits being used by the Nottingham police in the later 1920s, while the famous manufacturer himself was a regular Jaguar customer in his last years, owning an E-type at the time of his death in 1970. 1924 Swallow sidecars had pentagonal panelling in place of the octagonal layout of earlier models, and de luxe versions ran to luggage boots and safety-glass screens. Balloon tyres and left-handed lugs for Continental export followed shortly afterwards. If by 1927 other firms were copying the Lyons idiom, Swallow's superior experience enabled them to undercut such rivals as Hughes, Millford and Whitley by a good £2 a unit: they also steered clear of fabric covering when the Weymann craze spread to the motorcycle world. Swallow 'chairs' were used by some competitors in the 1924 and 1925 Sidecar TTs, scoring second and third places in the former event when attached to Dot and Matador machines ridden by Reed and Tinkler respectively. 1926 saw a move to bigger premises in Cocker Street, although in the meantime William Lyons, like many of his customers, was contemplating the next rung on the ladder – four wheels.

Way back in the autumn of 1922 Sir Herbert Austin, who had once infuriated

The sports model No 5 sidecar. Shaped like a torpedo and made of aluminium, it exudes the 1920s in every line

guests at a motorcycling dinner by calling the combination 'an unmechanical contraption', launched his concept of a perfect substitute, the celebrated Austin Seven. This has since become almost a joke, on the strength of its 'spit-and-hope' lubrication, uncertain and uncoupled four-wheel brakes, and savage clutch with infinitesimal travel, but by the standards of its day it offered civilized, dependable and quite rapid transportation for two adults and two children. It was what it claimed to be – a big car in miniature – and at £165 it cost no more than a well-equipped big-twin combination. The Baby Austin was an immediate best-seller, backed as it was by an impressive competition career, and it successfully underwrote the rest of the Austin range for a decade. What is more, its advent coincided with a change of direction in the special coachwork industry.

In the early days of the motor-car, ninety per cent of all vehicles were bespoke; in Europe, at any rate. Even firms with big outputs, such as FIAT and Renault, waited until the eve of the First World War before offering standardised styles, and these tended to be simple roadsters and touring cars, confined to the smaller chassis in a maker's range. Admittedly there were exceptions; the Lanchester brothers, who conceived their cars as entities and not just as frames for the bodies of others, maintained a coachwork department from the start. So did Daimler of Coventry. But in 1914 the car factories of Britain were backed by a multitude of coachbuilders, from the haute couture of London (Barker, Hooper, H J Mulliner, Windover) to provincial houses of no less repute who catered for conservative local taste. Liverpool had Lawton, Manchester several headed by Arnold and Cockshoot, East Anglia was served by Mann Egerton in Norwich and Botwood in Ipswich. Leicestershire drew on Hamshaw, and Yorkshire on Rippon of Huddersfield. Equally respected were Vincent in Reading, Marshalsea in Taunton and Angus-

17

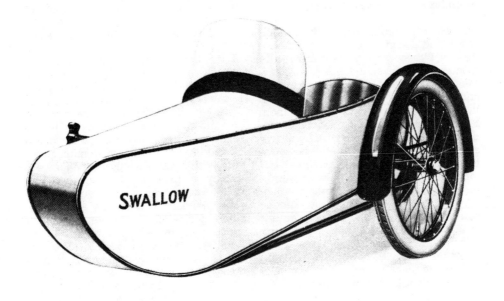

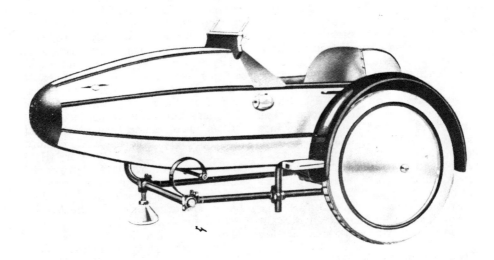

The semi-sports model No 7 sidecar. This was the conventional sporty single-seater which typified Swallow design until the late 1940s

Sanderson in Newcastle-upon-Tyne.

These firms made one-offs that were worthy successors to the horse-drawn carriages of an earlier era. Most of them were chauffeur-driven, too, though the Lady of the House would occasionally order a neat little cabriolet for her own use, mounted on one of the numerous 12hp 4-cylinder chassis turned out by British and Continental makers.

Post-war inflation, however, changed all this. Between 1914 and 1918 the native manufacturers turned to munitions, and the resultant invasion of cheap and stereotyped American cars had provided raw material which had to be 'customized' in order to render it bearable to the eye. By 1920 the camouflaging of that ungainly staple, the Model-T Ford, was a recognized industry: some coachbuilders, notably Gordon in Birmingham and Morris Russell in London, did it quite well. What is more, the traditionally bespoke was becoming expensive. In 1914 the list price of a Rolls-Royce Silver Ghost chassis was £985, and for £1,500 a customer could have a personable creation if he drove himself, while £400 more would cater for a chauffeur as well. Within a decade the going price for a complete 40-50hp Rolls had almost doubled.

Worse still for the individualist, mass-production methods had hit Europe. Citroën and Morris were the principal practitioners, but older firms such as FIAT of Italy and Opel of Germany had changed their images, and the result was dull, uninspired and boxy. It grew worse in 1925, when André Citroën made his first all-steel saloon. A maker might (as did Citroën) offer six or seven different styles on a basic chassis, but the result was still

The coupé sports de luxe model No 1 sidecar. Its aero-screen followed aircraft practice

lacking in beauty. The first closed Austin Sevens possessed a rectangular charm, it is true, but this appealed mainly to latter-day Vintage enthusiasts. In such a climate the packager must thrive, and the classic illustration of a packager's Utopia can be seen in post-1945 Italy. Here the man in the street either owned a FIAT or did without – and in the immediate post-war years his choice was limited to three types, according to his income and requirements. The consequence was a modern edition of William Lyons' early years. Coachbuilders started with special-bodied FIATs in series of a hundred or two (witness Pininfarina's 1100ES of 1950). Then, with the spread of unitary construction, they switched to buying FIAT mechanical elements and wedding them to their own hulls: and in the ultimate stage we encounter devices such as the Abarth, which bear little relation to anything emanating from the vast assembly-halls of Mirafiori.

As with post-Fascist Italy, so with Britain in the 1920s. Lyons was neither alone, nor was he a pioneer. The first SS was not unveiled until October 1931, nor was it promoted to the car section of a London show until 1934, ten years after Cecil Kimber had sold the first of his Morris-based MGs from the Morris Garages in Oxford. The MG was recognised as a make in its own right by 1927. Others were to follow, notably the Jensen brothers. Their first Avon Standard was on sale in 1929; four years later they had their own coachbuilding business, and in 1937 the successful Jensen Ford V8 had given way to a 3½-litre Jensen. Maybe it was still a Ford under the skin, but neither Dearborn nor Dagenham would have recognized it.

Nonetheless, the first Austin Swallow two-seater of 1927 was quite a car, and certainly the prettiest of a vast flood of special Baby Austins then on the market. Nothing was done to the chassis beyond strengthening the side-members with angle iron, but only the winged wheel badge on the radiator identified the end-product with Sir Herbert's master-

Swallow's skill in matching curves to the perpendicular is demonstrated by the 1930 Swift Ten Swallow. The bonnet line is unaltered from the stock saloons

piece. The bullnose shape of this component was matched by a bulbous tail housing tools and battery, and the Austin's combined head-side lamps on the scuttle were replaced by conventionally-mounted separate units. As first seen, the car had cycle-type wings turning with the wheels, and for an extra £10 (the list price was only £174) the buyer could have a detachable hardtop as well. By 1928 the Swallow had acquired full mudguarding, running boards, and a vee screen. By contrast with the stock Austin's sparsely furnished panel, the Lyons version was fully instrumented.

By 1928 the new car had made its mark, and chassis were being supplied from Birmingham in batches of fifty. An even better seller was the bulbous little saloon of 1929, which introduced the celebrated 'pen-nib' colour separation, so called because of the way the

two tones were combined on the bonnet top. The colours themselves also contrasted with the sombre navies, browns and maroons favoured in the later 1920s – what price such combinations as Nile blue/ivory, apple green/ivory, and cream/carnation red, all available in 1930 to tempt the ladies? At £187.50, this was a bargain: it was even more of one in 1932, when the price was down to £165, plus £1 for a coloured radiator muff, £1.75 for a coloured steering-wheel rim, £2.05 for a clock, and £2.45 for electric direction indicators. Also extra were dipping headlamps, incidentally!

These were years of expansion. Already in 1927 the firm's title had been changed to Swallow Sidecar and Coachbuilding Company, and three years later the 'Sidecar' was dropped from the name. Not that the old love was cast away, by a long chalk, for 500 a week were still being made in 1937, but thenceforward car bodies took precedence. Before the end of 1928 Lyons was established nearer his sources of supply, in a former munitions factory at Foleshill, Coventry. Another excellent contact, and one destined to last until the present day, was made with Henlys ('London's Leading Motor Agents') who undertook distribution of the Austin Swallow in the southern half of Britain, Parkers of Manchester taking the north. Henlys organised an impressive sales tour in April 1930, and repeated the experiment in 1932, after the introduction of the SS. Customers poured in, especially ladies, for where else could less than £200 buy anything so handy and chic, with a lady's companion built into the cubbyhole lid ?

Already Lyons and Walmsley were applying their talents to other popular makes. A Morris-Cowley Swallow two-seater at £210 in 1927 was encroaching too closely on Kimber's preserves to be viable, but an Austin-like saloon on the small overhead-camshaft FIAT 509A chassis (1929) did better, even if the low roof-line was won at the price of impaired vision, and FIAT dropped this model from their range soon after the Swallow version was announced. A similar body was applied to 150 or so 10hp Swifts in 1930 and 1931, this venture coming to an abrupt halt when Swift went broke. Inevitably Lyons tried his luck with that answer to the custom coachbuilder's prayer, the 1,271cc 6-cylinder Wolseley Hornet introduced during the 1930 season. Here was the perfect woman's car, smooth as only a six could be, and so flexible that gear-changing was all but eliminated. (The model's manifold failings displayed themselves only to enthusiastic drivers who soon discovered not only that it did not hold the road but was only too willing to rev its guts out!) For this chassis Swallow produced both a modernized version of the original Austin two-seater theme and a neat four-seater which anticipated the first open SS of 1933. These Wolseley Swallow bodies were perhaps the prettiest of a prolific crop of semi-bespoke bodies (nineteen by early 1932), and were subsequently applied to the Hornet Special, a sports model which Wolseley introduced that year. This latter variant was destined to outlive the other 'packaged' products of

Foleshill, surviving into 1933, at which time the four-seater at £260 was actually cheaper than the regular Daytona version handled by Eustace Watkins, Wolseley's London distributor. Already people were asking how William Lyons did it, even if operations were still on a modest scale, with a maximum output of thirty bodies a day in 1931, and paint-and-varnish was just beginning to give way to cellulose.

Alongside the Austins, FIATs and Swifts, however, Swallow had gone to work on another marque which was to decide their future, the Standard. As seen at the 1929 London Show, the curvaceous lines of Lyons' Big Nine sports saloon did not blend well with Standard's traditional shouldered radiator, but by the time the public got their hands on this one (at £250, only £35 more than was asked for an ordinary car with factory body), it had been tidied up. What is more, the rounded-vee radiator not only anticipated the original SS shape, but was copied by Standard for their 1931 range.

The Standard Nine had little performance potential, but alongside it Captain J P Black, having rescued his company from the doldrums, had introduced a second string in the form of a solid seven-bearing side-valve six. Never a best-seller, the 6-cylinder Standard had an excellent reputation for reliability, and was the next logical step for Lyons, who liked this type of engine, but had no use for fussy miniatures such as the Wolseley Hornet. In any case, it is hard to see what other car he could have chosen. Austin's Sixteen was heavy, adamantine and durable, while the bigger 16hp Wolseley, though it boasted an overhead-camshaft engine, was designed to use the bodies of the big 21-60hp model, and was consequently overweight. The first 6-cylinder Swallow saloon was announced in May 1931.

Once again there were no mechanical modifications, and only the longer bonnet distinguished the 16hp from its 4-cylinder counterpart. 60mph was about its limit, but at £275 it was yet

another bargain. For curvaceous elegance nobody minded paying £30 over
the price of the regular Standard, and at
the same time the Swallow was quite a
lot cheaper than its contemporary, the
Avon Swan coupé designed by the
Jensens, and already 'doctored' to in-
corporate flatter springs, a lower
radiator and a raked steering column.

Requirements were, however,
changing. MGs were fast shedding their
more obvious Morris affiliations, and
even if the popular little 847cc Midget
was Kimber's bread-and-butter, he had
scored a minor success with the $2\frac{1}{2}$-litre
'18-80' based on the ohc Morris Isis.
Somehow this one, like all the big MGs
right up to the 'C' of the 1960s, never
quite made it. The three-speed Morris
box of the Mk Is sorted ill with the rest
of the specification, and the MG Six
was not particularly cheap at £545. Seen
through later eyes it looks a sober
aristocrat beside the flashy 1932 SS,
but it was too costly to sell well during
the depression.

Lyons' new recipe was an extension
of the policy which had brought him to
the front of the packaging industry in
four hectic years: a specialist car using
well-tried ingredients and individual
styling, which could be sold at a price
competitive enough to warrant the full
cooperation of his chosen suppliers.
This way he could circumvent the
handicaps of building on a completely
stock chassis designed for the utility
market. FIATs, Swifts and Standards
had perpetuated the 'long, low look'
(you could not do much with the Austin
Seven!), but only at the price of claustrophobic vision. What was needed was
an underslung frame.

**The missing link. By 1930 the
Standard Big Nine had joined the
Swallow range, and a new–style
radiator had been designed for it**

September 1931 was a singularly
inauspicious time for any automobile
novelty. Morris' Hundred-Pound Minor
had proved a damp squib, and
Austin's Twelve-Six had tarnished the
reputation of Britain's Dependable Car.
Bentley, Arrol-Johnston and Swift had
gone to the wall, and Star were soon to
follow suit. Lanchester had been swal-
lowed by Daimler, and the English
end of the once-proud Sunbeam-Talbot-
Darracq combine was kept alive only
by Roesch's brilliantly-engineered Talbots. Rover could still sell their range
in 1931, but there was nothing in their
catalogue that would rate as 'One of
Britain's Fine Cars'. Ramsay MacDonald
had let the country slip off the Gold
Standard, and new-car registrations had
reached their nadir. Only Black at
Standards was on the up-and-up.

With the announcement of his 1932
range came some 4- and 6-cylinder
Swallow variants incorporating the
latest modifications, which meant four
forward speeds and Bendix Duo-
Servo brakes. The Wolseleys and
Austins were likewise continued, while
the sidecars came in duo-tone finish.
There was also some tantalising publicity: 'SS is the name of a new car
that's going to thrill the hearts of the
motoring public, and the trade alike.
It's something utterly new . . . different
. . . better. Long . . . low . . . very low . . .
and very FAST! At the Show, or before,
two SS coupés of surpassing beauty will
be presented. WAIT . . . THE SS IS
COMING!'

With Adolf Hitler eighteen months
away from power, the initials had no
sinister connotation. Nor was their
meaning apparent – it was not intended
to be, and it was never revealed
whether they stood for Swallow Sports,
Swallow Special, Standard Swallow, or
any other apposite combination. The
public was apathetic: if they had not
laid their cars up to wait for the economic climate to improve, they were
certainly not thinking of a new one. And
if they were, the Depression was no
time to try a new make.

How wrong they all were!

SS TO JAGUAR

William Lyons was no man to be discouraged by a Depression. The SS took its bow at Olympia in that dark autumn of 1931.

Even now the world is not quite sure what it thinks about the first car to bear the name. There was many an unkind interpretation of those cryptic initials, the American writer Ralph Stein termed it an 'excruciatingly rakish little sedan', while the motoring bard W H Charnock, who bought a tourer for his honeymoon in 1933, later alluded to it as 'a real cad's car'. Yet surviving examples are eagerly hunted (at least two survive behind the Iron Curtain in Czechoslovakia) and the Classic Car Club of America has set its seal of approval on the early side-valve sixes, though of the pushrod species only the SS 100 is recognised.

Nor was the SS I quite the novelty it purported to be. The 'long, low look' had been introduced to a startled world in 1929 on C W van Ranst's L29 Cord, a device which thanks to its front-wheel drive gave an impression of length beyond its seventeen-odd feet. Mechanically the Cord was an unsatisfactory improvisation, but it struck a new note in styling, and two years later almost the whole American industry had followed suit, the 1931 8-cylinder Chryslers being particularly successful. The SS, however, was the idiom's first British application, and in its original guise it emerged as a rakish coupé with the fashionable landau irons on its rear quarters, yards and yards of bonnet, helmet-type cycle wings, and a relatively deep windscreen, which offered adequate vision at the price of a slight resemblance to a dog-kennel. Thanks to the use of an underslung frame, it stood only fifty-five inches off the ground, thirteen inches less than the regular Standard Sixteen saloon.

The mechanical ingredients, likewise, were pure Standard, though the

The £1,000 (or $5,000) look, as worn by the first SS I coupé, 1932. The early radiator shell was much narrower than on subsequent models

chassis differed in more than one respect from normal Standard practice. The wheelbase was three inches longer than that of the Sixteen, the front springs were mounted outside the frame, and the engine was set back seven inches to accentuate the sports-car look, an effect achieved on the Cord by mounting the gearbox out front. The 2.1-litre engine and its four-speed gearbox were unmodified, the former developing an adequate 48bhp, while top-gear performance was improved by using the higher of Standard's two optional axle ratios (4.66:1). The axles and Marles cam-and-lever steering gear were entirely stock, though early in the model's career buyers willing to pay £10 extra were able to specify the more powerful $2\frac{1}{2}$-litre Twenty engine. The additional performance was, however, balanced by the higher tax chargeable in Britain – £4 per annum. All this sold for an astonishing £310; as a second string there was the SS II, a miniature version based on Standard's smallest model, the 1,052cc Little Nine. This sold for £210 and was distinguishable by its shallower windscreen and painted radiator shell: that of the SS I was heavily chromium-plated.

It was also an over-statement to describe the new car as 'very, very fast', even when one reflects that mile-a-minute speeds were still well beyond the capabilities of Family Tens and Twelves in 1931. The new generation of medium-sized 6-cylinder saloons – Morris's Oxford-Six, Hillman's Wizard, and the Standard on which the SS was based – were working hard at 60mph. Cars of the calibre of the $4\frac{1}{2}$-litre Invicta and Roesch's new Talbot 105 could approach 100mph, but the latter cost £750, and the former appreciably more. Viewed by such standards the new SS's 71mph was respectable, especially when 60 came up easily on the close-ratio third, and 55 could be maintained all day without fatigue. Despite the car's subsequent reputation for running out of road, a contemporary writer felt that it was 'very steady on bends and corners . . .

A 1934 SS I tourer, seen in a British 'trial'

giving the driver a feeling of complete confidence in its stability'. The cable-operated brakes would stop the SS in a remarkable 29 feet from 30mph, and the liberal use of Standard components reduced servicing costs to a minimum. The '£1,000 look' proved to be more than just a pretty face, as witness deliveries of 771 units in the SS's first season. Among early customers was Jim Mollison, then the golden boy of British civil aviation. Stage stars discovered the SS soon afterwards. George Formby, the Lancashire comedian, bought one in 1933.

1933 models had a lower roofline which improved appearance, though once again at the expense of forward vision. Engines were now more powerful, the Sixteen developing 50bhp,

while other weaknesses of the original cars were tackled. A more efficient radiator block coped with overheating, and an armoured bulkhead with the seepage of fumes into the cockpit, an occupational hazard of cramped underbonnet space. Frames were re-inforced with cruciform bracing, and were also lengthened (wheelbase went up from 112 to 119 inches). The new full-flow wings and running-boards gave the car a tidier look, and the 1933 coupés were four-seaters. The twin armchair-type rear seats added a sybaritic touch: they were also essential since the propeller shaft intruded too far to allow of any other arrangement.

Performance, likewise, was up. The Sixteen did 75mph and 20mpg, and the Twenty recorded 81.82mph on test as well as taking only fifteen seconds to reach 60mph: good by the standards of the day, though a modern 4.2-litre

XJ6 Jaguar does it in a fraction over ten seconds.

1933 was also to see a determined challenge from another breed of not-quite-standard Standard, the special-bodied type marketed by Avon of Warwick. Since the departure of the Jensens, C F Beauvais had taken over as their stylist, and his treatment of the theme was less exaggerated, the tourers being especially handsome. Further, 6-cylinder Avons boasted high-compression heads and RAG carburetters similar to those found on SS cars of the 1933-35 period. They came in three body styles at a time when Lyons still marketed only his basic coupé, and they were slightly cheaper. Avon's interests also extended down the Standard range to the Big Nine originally favoured by Swallow in 1930, and to the unfortunate 6-cylinder Little Twelve. There was little to choose between the rival strains in all-out performance, either. Alas for Warwick, the underslung frame remained a Lyons exclusive, and subsequent Avons became less and less sporting in character. The last of the line, a saloon and a drophead coupé on Standard's Flying Twenty chassis offered in 1937, cost more than the 2½-litre SS Jaguar and were strictly for *Concours d'Elégance.*

In any case, by the spring of 1933 SS had moved in on Avon's preserve with a handsome sports tourer of their own. One of the first of these won its class in that year's Scottish Rally, a step beyond previous 'competition' successes. These had so far been confined to *Concours* such as Bristol, Ramsgate and Eastbourne, not to mention an award won by an SSI/Car Cruiser outfit in the Junior Car Club's Caravan Rally, for 'the caravan equipped by its owner in the most useful and ingenious way'. (For serious road work, of course, such an ensemble would have presented appalling problems of vision and manipulation.) But those who dismissed the SS as a promenade car were surprised to see the entry of a works team in that toughest of rallies, the International Alpine Trial. For this Lyons chose experienced drivers,

A proud owner takes delivery of his new SS I saloon, 1934. The horns, wheel trims and plated spare wheel cover were factory equipment

Rarest of the SS Is is the 1935 drop-head coupé, made for only a few months. Some were sold in New York

Humfrey Symons, Miss Margaret Allan and C M Needham, who had done well in 1932 with an Invicta.

This was a gallant failure. In the tortuous passes of the Alps steering which stiffened up on full lock was a grievous disadvantage, and cooling arrangements admirable for ordinary road work could not take the extra strain. Two of the cars retired with blown head gaskets, only Needham finishing, and then an indifferent eighth

in his class, though the private owner Koch redeemed things a little with his sixth place. Nonetheless, SS were back in 1934 : this time the engines were too new and tight, and suffered from head distortion, but a third place in the Team Event was creditable when one reflects upon the cars that beat them, the celebrated Roesch Talbots and the equally well prepared 6-cylinder Adlers from Germany.

Sales improved steadily : 1,525 in 1933

Even the handsome tourer looked stunted on the 4-cylinder SS II chassis

and 1,793 in 1934, when the SS Car Club was formed. In this latter year Standards lengthened the piston strokes of their 6-cylinder engines, and the SS followed suit, the Twenty emerging with a capacity of 2,664cc (73 x 106mm), dimensions which were to apply to all 2½-litre units until the demise of this line in 1951. Other improvements included bigger brake drums, a new gearbox with synchromesh on the three upper ratios, Silentbloc spring shackles, self-cancelling direction indicators, and a reversing lamp. At the same time the hexagonal SS emblem (an answer to

cost only £345 at a time when a comparable Talbot 105 sold for £795 and Alvis's Speed Twenty for £825.

New faces appeared at Foleshill. In 1934 E W Rankin was recruited to take care of publicity, and 1935 saw the arrival of William Heynes from Humber as chief engineer. At the same time, incidentally, William Walmsley severed his connections with the firm.

The 1935 SS Is were even better, twin RAG carburetters, bigger sumps, high-lift camshafts and higher axle ratios being among the season's improvements. The year's new crop of

MG's octagon, devised by a Mr Reavesby of the Iliffe magazine group) made its appearance, as did a third body style. This was a sports saloon less claustrophobic than the basic coupé. Equipment was comprehensive: the dashboard contained a clock and a thermometer as well as the usual instruments, there was an opening rear window complete with remotely-controlled blind, and SS Is were available in fifteen different colours, not to mention nineteen combinations of paint and trim. And still the most expensive model – the saloon with 20hp engine –

The Hon Brian Lewis (Lord Essendon) with the SS 90 prototype, 1935. The sloping tail differed from the SS 100 style of production models

factory extras included built-in jacks, metallic finish, and Philco radio, at £19.80 including fitting. The original coupé was dropped, but to take its place were two fresh styles, the Airline saloon and a drophead of which only a handful were made. Airlines carried their spare wheels in the front wings, allowing more room for luggage in the swept tails, an improvement on the

29

Three generations of styling at a 1936 SS Car Club meet: the '34 coupé with blind rear quarters and landau irons, the slinky '35 Airline, and (second row left) a very early 2½-litre Jaguar saloon

top-opening boxes of the saloons and coupés.

Meanwhile the SS II continued as a very junior partner. Its styling had been left unaltered in 1933, when it acquired a four-speed gearbox, but the changes of subsequent seasons had all been applied. 1934 and later cars were also larger and more powerful, being available with either Standard's 1.3-litre Ten or the bigger 1,608cc Twelve unit. From the summer of 1934 onward there was a tourer model as well, this being the first Lyons-built car to enter the service

of the police: the Bolton Force took delivery of one that September.

Somehow the SS II never really caught on. Sales were a mere 1,796 as against well over 4,000 of the 6-cylinder cars, and this in spite of the tax-consciousness of Britons. For one thing, the 'long, low look' does not take kindly to foreshortening, and the SS II looked just as stunted as had Chrysler's smaller 1931 creations. It was also, unlike its bigger sisters, up against formidable and well-entrenched opposition. In the medium-sized class, William Lyons' bargain offerings were giant-killers and incredible value for money; among their victims were to be numbered not only MG's rival pushrod sixes, but also Anglo-Americans of the stamp of the Railton, and even cars like the Armstrong Siddeley and the Alvis, which appealed to a totally different type of customer, yet themselves competed against the Jaguar in their declining years. When it came to small luxury fours of sporting mien, however, he could not compete with Riley's excellent Nine, the Triumph Gloria, or even the rather bogus Hillman Aero Minx purveyed by the Rootes Group. The 10hp SS was heavy at 21cwt, it was slow, and even in price it was undercut by the Hillman, though at £265 it was cheaper than either Riley or Triumph.

1935 saw more rally successes, but the Heynes influence was being felt, and in March a further step was taken in the direction of a real sports car. The SS 90 retained the old side-valve 20hp unit, but with the aid of a 7:1 compression ratio output was raised to 90bhp, and the shortened chassis carried a simple and well-proportioned two-seater body terminating in one of the fashionable 'Le Mans-type' slab tanks. Gear ratios were high and close, and as always the new model was excellent value at £395, even if the 100mph speedometer was a trifle optimistic. Only twenty-three of these cars were made before the switch to overhead valves for 1936.

In September 1935 SS Cars Ltd was floated as a public company, a new subsidiary being formed to handle the sidecar activities, which were not sold to the Helliwell Group until after the war. But the same month saw a far more

'Wardour Street Bentley.' A 1936 2½-litre Jaguar saloon competes in a British rally. Wheel discs were a fashionable extra

The baby Jaguar of 1936 had the splendid proportions of its big sister, but the 1,608cc side-valve Standard engine made 70mph hard work.

important development, the first of the Jaguar line.

The SS I had been a 'non-standard Standard'. Such a term could never be applied to the 2½-litre SS Jaguar, even if its seven-bearing 6-cylinder engine and four-speed synchromesh gearbox were still made in Standard's Canley factory. Further, the top end of this unit was entirely new; the ohv head was the work of Heynes, assisted by Harry Weslake, and output went up to an impressive 104bhp, sufficient for a 90mph saloon. The old side-valve unit had only touched these heights when allied to light two-seater bodywork. Some people looked askance at the light-alloy connecting-rods, but though these have been known to wilt in old age, the new pushrod SS engine proved to be extremely durable, mileages of

200,000 between major overhauls being not unknown. The twin SU carburetters were fed by an electric pump (an option on SS Is since 1934) and the old Standard chassis was replaced by an entirely new cruciform-braced box-section affair, made for SS by Rubery Owen: this was underslung at the rear only. On a 119-inch wheelbase the new Jaguar saloon measured only 178 inches from stem to stern. Weight was up 5cwt on the SS I, but power was going up faster, and independent road-test reports revealed a two-way maximum speed of 86mph, an 0-50mph acceleration time of twelve seconds, and handling far superior to that of any previous model from Foleshill. The rod-operated Girling brakes gave 'powerful yet smooth control', and the synchromesh box came in for high praise.

The body of the new model had acquired a dignity to match the smartness of earlier models. The four-door close-coupled sports saloon had a balanced elegance reminiscent of the £1,500 Park Ward Bentley, and the motoring journalists who gathered at the Jaguar's launching party guessed the price, on appearance alone, to be nearly £700. William Lyons, however, sold it for an impossible £385. It rode on centre-lock wire wheels, while the radiator grille had been simplified. The result was unmistakably a Jaguar, and the XJ6s which rub shoulders with the company's magnificently-restored 1936 saloon in the factory showroom preserve a lineal affinity.

This was the star of the range, but also offered were a tourer and a 100 two-seater with the 2.7-litre ohv engine and styling little changed from 1935. A smaller version of the Jaguar idiom was the 1½-litre at £285, though this one continued to use the sv 12hp Standard engine and made little impression. The SSI and SS II saloons were continued for another year with Jaguar-shaped radiator shells.

A distinctive car must have a distinctive name, and a zoological one was the obvious choice. 'Jaguar' had reached the short list when somebody remembered that the nearby Armstrong Siddeley factory had made a successful radial aero-engine of that name in the 1920s: a telephone call to Siddeley's Parkside works soon sorted out the problem, so 'Jaguar' it was, though as yet the cars retained the SS marque-name, and the big predator featured only in the company's colour advertisements. The famous mascot did not appear until 1937, and then only after an accessory firm had marketed something which Bill Rankin, an amateur sculptor of some distinction, likened to 'a cat shot off a fence'. He countered with an anatomically-correct jaguar, which was then stylised by *Autocar* artist Frederick Gordon-Crosby. Like everything the SS company made, the emblem was excellent value for money (£2.10 when first introduced) but it remained an extra until the advent of the Mk VIII in 1957.

Early in the spring of 1936 the 100 models started to appear. These have become something of a legend in recent years, since Americans have shown themselves willing to pay $7000 and over for well-restored examples. The 100 has always been rare: only 309 were produced of both types, the original 2½-litre and the later '3½' were made between 1936 and 1940. The 1936 cars used the regular 104bhp engine, and 92mph was about the limit in standard trim. 60 could be reached in 13½ seconds. Much has been made of the 100's skittish behaviour at high speeds (on London's tricky Crystal Palace circuit the model's gyrations were notorious), its ferocious tyre consumption, and poor steering lock (which last did not, in the event, stop it doing extremely well in rallies). Its strong suits were functional elegance, simplicity, and freedom from temperament: like the saloons, it could return 21mpg and better, and it could outperform anything in its price class, not to mention most things outside. The 100's great rival in Britain was the advanced 2-litre Type-328 BMW from Germany. Sophisticated, aerodynamically bodied, and blessed with independently sprung front wheels and hydraulic brakes, it was the XK Jaguar of its day. It also retailed at £695 – or £300 more than the SS.

The model was never seriously raced, but a Brooklands lap speed of 104.41mph running stripped is a fair yardstick of its performance. SS 100s won the 1937 RAC and Welsh Rallies outright, annexed their classes in both events in 1938, and repeated this latter performance in the 1939 'Welsh'. There was also a class victory in the 1938 Paris-Nice Trial, while even more remarkable was Tommy Wisdom's best individual performance irrespective of class in the 1936 International Alpine Trial, which more than avenged the humiliations of 1933. In 1948 Ian Appleyard's 3½-litre scored a class win in the 'Alpine', other post-war triumphs being recorded at hill-climbs such as Bo'ness, Craigantlet and Prescott. Even in 1949, on the eve of the XK era, Appleyard's car was still good for a second place in the Dutch Tulip Rally.

By late 1936, the 2½-litre SS Jaguar was accounting for nearly ninety per. cent of all new British registrations in the 20hp taxation class (a victory at Standard's expense!), and the cars moved on into 1937 with only minor changes, a policy vindicated by record deliveries of 3,554 units. What happened in 1938, however, amounted to far more than a face-lift.

The most significant development was the adoption of all-metal bodies in place of the composite structures inherited from Swallow days. Closed bodies were re-styled with five inches more of internal length and appreciably more width, while spare wheels were removed from the front wings to the boot (an attempt to mount them in the boot lid was soon abandoned as being clumsy). The two regular styles – the saloon and a new foursome drophead coupé – were standardised throughout a range which now included three models, two of them entirely new. Only the 2½-litre was continued.

The lethargic side-valve 1½-litre was replaced by a new pushrod '1½' using a 1,776cc unit based on the Standard Fourteen, while at the top of the range was a brand-new 82 x 110mm 3½-litre six developing 125bhp. The engine design paralleled that of the '2½' except for the provision of an automatic choke. The result was performance in the Bentley class to match Bentley looks, and in short-chassis 100 guise Lyons had produced something electrifying. Top speed was a genuine 100mph, and it was almost as quick to 60mph as a 1971 XJ6. A stock example did a standing lap of Brooklands Track at 86mph and, with the aid of a 12½:1 compression and a 3:1 back axle, a specially tuned model was persuaded to lap the course at 118mph. All this cost only £445, or £20 less than the most expensive Jaguar – the 3½-litre coupé. No wonder that the firm had pushed their weekly output up to 150 cars by the summer.

Not that this rationalisation was without its headaches. Production of the new all-steel bodies took some time to

get off the ground, and the 1½-litre suffered from having to haul coachwork designed for bigger and faster machinery. Its genuine 70mph took a long, straight road to attain. On the credit side it was the bargain of the season at £298, lacked none of the elegance of its bigger sisters, could run up to nearly 60mph on its close-ratio third gear, and possessed an excellent cruising range thanks to its fourteen-gallon tank. Pound for pound, it was a much better proposition than the VA-type MG at £325, and probably did more to kill the bigger pushrod cars from Abingdon than did its companion sixes. It was also destined to be William Lyons' first real volume-seller, with nearly 13,000 delivered between 1938 and 1949. Furthermore the new 3½-litre effectively cut the ground from under Kimber's 2.6-litre WA-type MG of 1939, though there was little to choose between the two marques on handling, and the

The SS Car Club team for the 1937 Welsh Rally. Perched on the centre car is the late Bill Rankin, the company's Public Relations Officer

MG's hydraulic brakes were superior to the Jaguar's Girlings. MG had already given up the unequal struggle before Hitler marched into Poland, and their 1941 saloon-car offering would have been the little 1,250cc YA-type which eventually reached the public six years later. This, incidentally, placed the Octagon up against easier game in the shape of the Rootes Group's Hillman-based Sunbeam-Talbots.

Thanks to Hitler, the 1938 SS models were destined for a ten-year currency. There were improvements in 1940 and again in 1945, as well as a change of name and some further simplifications of the range, but the shape survived until the advent of Mk V at the 1948 Earls Court Show. 1940 improvements amounted to heaters (optional on the 1½-litre and regular equipment on the sixes) and piston-type dampers on the bigger models. A pound was also knocked off the price of a factory-fitted radio, though this was scarcely relevant: music while one drove was soon to become illegal under the Defence Regulations.

Production was allowed to work itself out in the first months of the Second World War, but in that last incomplete year of 1939 SS Cars Ltd had broken all records, with deliveries of 5,378 cars. William Lyons was still only thirty-eight years old but he commanded a workforce of 1,000 men and women, and a factory that could turn out 200 vehicles a week. Perhaps the finest compliment came from the Luftwaffe, who had taken the trouble to photograph Foleshill in June 1939, and were to reap the reward of their espionage in the great Coventry blitz seventeen months later.

Above: SS 100 in characteristic attitude on the start line, Lewes Speed
Trials, 1939 Below: SS 100 involved in one of those embarrassing
gyrations, the Three Hours Sports Car Race, Brooklands, 1938
Right: SS 100 storming Prescott Hill at the 1939 International Meeting

Above: The 1939 Jaguar drophead coupé was still a promenade car despite its 90mph. The girl, the sea front, and the metallic finish all evoke a more leisured era of rallying

Above right: The state of the art, 1939. A 3½-litre saloon outside the factory, looking far more expensive than its list price of £445 ($2,225). Below: Nostalgia: the helmeted girl in her SS 100, the hand-operated pumps at the filling station, and the stoneguards of the big headlamps. Evidently between 1936 and 1939. Below right: The 3½-litre SS 100 coupé exhibited at the last prewar London Show, 1938, but never put into production

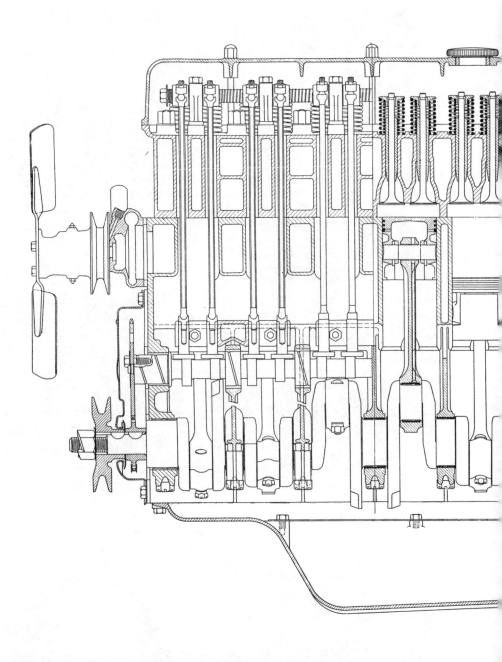

General Arrangement of SS 2½ litre engine
bore and stroke 73 mm x 106 mm

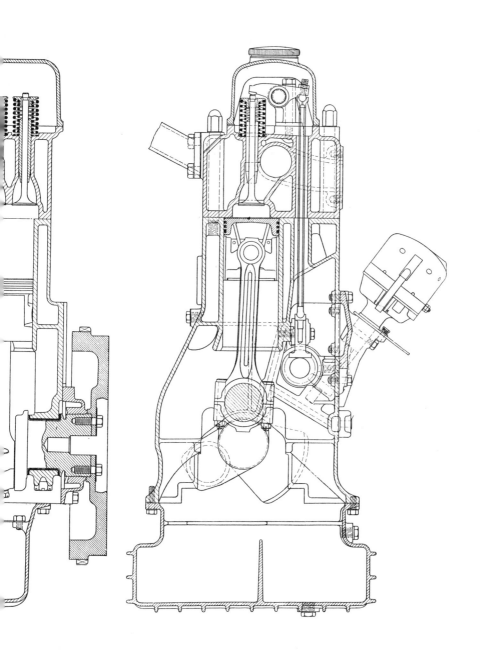

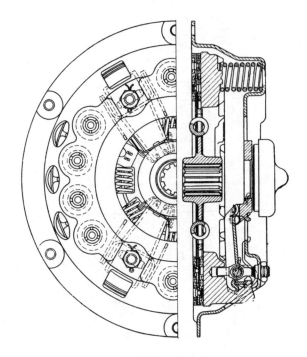

The clutch

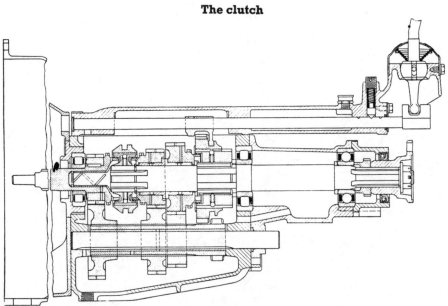

Four speed gear box

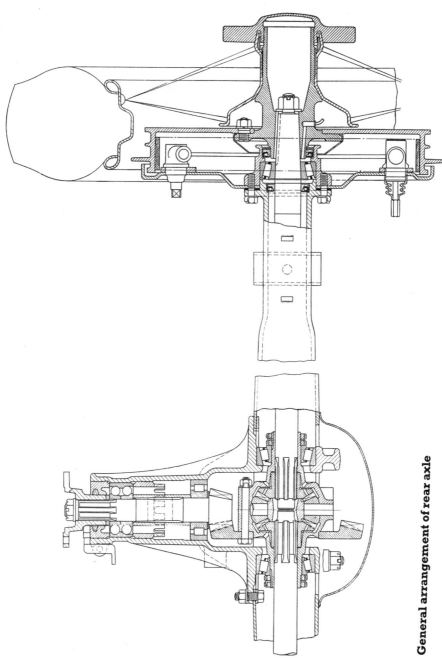

General arrangement of rear axle

THE XK STORY

In October 1945, after an interval of nearly six years, the first post-war Jaguar rolled off the lines at Foleshill.

Discriminating observers would have noticed few differences from 1940, apart from a new wording on the radiator badge, and the replacement of Reavesby's hexagon on the rear bumper by a monogrammed 'J'. An Extraordinary General Meeting of the company convened the previous March had decided to say goodbye to SS. The initials had acquired an unhappy connotation during the years of the Third Reich.

Foleshill's war had been closely tied up with the aircraft industry, through the production of components for Stirlings,

The XK 120 used by Leslie Johnson
and Stirling Moss to average over
170mph for 24 hours at Montlhéry

Lancasters, Spitfires, Oxfords, and another Big Cat, Armstrong Siddeley's Cheetah engine. Whitley and Wellington bombers had been repaired, and an old tradition had been maintained by large-scale manufacture of box side-cars and lightweight trailers for the army. There had also been a braco of interesting cross-country prototypes in the airborne Jeep idiom evolved by C W L Baily and Walter Hassan, the latter having joined SS in 1939 after making his name with such Brooklands 'specials' as the 8-litre Bentley-based Barnato-Hassan and the Bugatti-engined BHW. Neither of these engaging miniatures went into production: Type-VA used the 1,100cc vee-twin JAP engine

beloved of motorcycle makers, and Type-VB the familiar Ford Ten. Both, however, anticipated later Jaguar practice, with the unitary construction of the 1956 2.4-litre and the all-independent springing of the 1961 E-type.

If as yet there were no new models in the Jaguar range, the decks were being cleared for action. Sidecars no longer fitted into the picture, so the Swallow division was sold off: its successors, ironically enough, were to try their luck with cars again in 1954, but their Triumph-based Doretti lasted only a short while. More important, Lyons took a further step in the direction of manufacture by acquiring from Black of Standard all the machinery used in the production of the 6-cylinder engines. 1½-litre units still came from Standard; a mutual convenience, since Black had found a use for the 14hp ohv type in the first of his Triumphs, the '1800' roadster and razor-edge saloon.

Only saloons were offered by Jaguar in 1946, though the 6-cylinder drop-head coupés were reinstated exclusively for export at the end of 1947. Mechanical changes were limited to hypoid rear axles, and 2LS Girling brakes and Metalastik crankshaft dampers on the 'sixes'. Unusual in the prevailing atmosphere of austerity was a choice of seven exterior colours, but inflation and purchase tax played havoc with prices, which ranged from £684 for a standard 1½-litre up to £991 for a 3½-litre. Frightening by the standards of 1939, but even more so (in a different sense) when one reflects that in 1971 the simplest XJ-type retails for £2,398. Even in the first post-war season exports amounted to twenty-six per cent, and the first consignment of 3½-litres crossed the Atlantic in January 1947: so home customers at the back of the queue had to buy second-hand. And Lyons' products held their value, costing for example £825 for a 1939 1½-litre, £495 for a 1936 2½-litre, and

45

£385 for a 1935 SS I.

While Heynes and his team worked on the real post-war models, the wheels had to be kept turning, and they were. Only once, in the reconversion year of 1946, did the Jaguar balance-sheets show a loss, and over £100,000 was spent on new machine tools in 1947 alone. Some old traditions were observed, among them the hand-rubbing of bodies and the 'Clapham Junction' method of assembly whereby coachwork and chassis, irrespective of model, were offered up to each other at a single point on the line; this arrangement survived the adoption of unitary structures in 1956, complete hulls being wedded thereafter to the mechanical elements. Lyons now employed 1,500 hands, but Jaguar were never over-officered. It was said that every executive had at least two jobs to fulfil, and even in 1947 the managing director (William Lyons) doubled as sales manager.

The late 1940s and early 1950s were, of course, the perfect seller's market. A

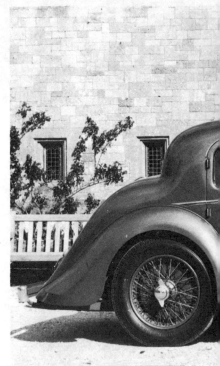

Ford-powered Jaguar. The VB-type Jeep of 1945 was the work of the Baily Hassan team

car-starved Europe had to re-equip; America was just discovering the fascination of foreign imports; and Britain, restricted to a small quota, would take anything it could get, which as far as Jaguars were concerned meant the frugal 1½-litre, since the 3½-litre's 17mpg thirst was out of place in a period of stringent petrol rationing. The problem was not to sell cars; it was to keep the production lines moving. Everything was in short supply – steel, coal and electricity – and these shortages set at naught an excellent record of labour relations backed by incentive bonuses. (In the days before the Society of Motor Manufacturers and Traders issued a breakdown of production figures by make, industrial spies anxious to discover how many cars Jaguar were making used to base their calculations on the weekly bonus

earned by individual workers!) The hard winter of 1946/7 was nearly a disaster. In February a fire destroyed all the company's stocks of soft trim, and though normal working was resumed after the ensuing weekend, seven days later the coal ran out and Jaguar's had to close altogether. By March everything was running smoothly again, but prices were forced up, a 1½-litre now costing £865. In the spring of 1948 the price was increased again, to £953. But somehow, in those first three seasons of Crippsian austerity, 9,660 Jaguars were delivered.

What did the future hold? Jaguar were now firmly established, but they could not continue indefinitely as they were, turning out traditional motorcars with beam axles and mechanical brakes. Other factories had new designs; Rolls-Royce, Bentley and Armstrong

The 1947 2½-litre Jaguar, hard to distinguish from its SS counterpart of 1938–40

1951 XK 120 Jaguar Coupé

Transitional Jaguars. Mk Vs had raked screens, heavier rear quarters and wheel parts. Most were saloons: the handsome coupés were reserved for export

Siddeley had been quick off the mark, and 1948 had seen true post-war models from Austin, Rootes, Singer and Vauxhall. Nor had Foleshill yet returned to the sports car market: though the 100 had figured in Jaguar's preliminary 1945 catalogue, only one example (Ian Appleyard's) had actually been built since VJ-Day.

But it was not until August 1948, a bare three months before the first post-war Earls Court Show, that any signs were forthcoming from Jaguar, and even then it was only a small pointer. When Colonel 'Goldie' Gardner attacked 2-litre international rec-

ord in his famous MG streamliner, EX 135, on Belgium's Jabbeke-Aeltre motorway, there was a twin-overhead camshaft 4-cylinder engine by Jaguar under its bonnet. A further clue was the impending demise of the faithful 1½-litre saloon. Standard-Triumph were rationalising their range, and henceforward the stylish Triumphs would use the engine and gearbox from the 2.1-litre Standard Vanguard. And this meant that all future Jaguars were to have Jaguar-built power units.

A month later the 2½-litre and 3½-litre Jaguars were offered in revised MkV form. (Many people, incidentally, refer to the beam-axle models of 1946/8 as 'MkIVs', but this designation has never been recognised by the factory). This transitional type soon replaced the 1½-litre as a home-market staple, as is indicated by the high proportion (8,787

out of 11,500) of 2½-litre variants in the total; this in spite of the smaller car's reluctance to exceed 85mph, whereas a good 3½-litre was 10mph faster and could see the 'ton' in favourable conditions. Engine and gearbox were virtually unchanged, but the chassis was entirely new, being a deep box-section affair on which the side-members were arched over the rear axle. The result was better ground clearance (earlier Jaguars were liable to bottom in 'colonial' conditions) but it also gave MkV a bows-down attitude which accentuated the heavy look conferred by sixteen-inch disc wheels. There was independent front suspension, by wishbones and torsion bars with Girling telescopic dampers, and the 2LS Girling brakes were hydraulically actuated. They felt a trifle spongy, but worked well, which is more than

could be said of the umbrella-handle handbrake, a device never repeated in this form on subsequent Jaguars. The traditional body shape acquired thinner screen pillars and detachable spats covered the rear wheels. Steering was low-geared; a 3½-litre tested in 1949 required four-and-a-half turns from lock to lock.

Opinions differ on MkV. Its handling was inferior, both to the last beam-axle cars and also to the big MkVII which followed it. One long-term owner has written: 'Fast cornering requires fairly brutal techniques, and I do not recommend MkV for rally driving tests, though it is surprising how quickly it can be wound round a tight corner.' In spite of which the Irishman Cecil Vard managed third place overall in the 1951 Monte Carlo Rally, Jaguar's best performance to date in that event. Everyone, however, agreed about the pushrod engine's proverbial reliability, which endeared it to police forces. One 2½-litre of my acquaintance averaged 22mpg over 17,000 miles. A drophead coupé was offered as well as the saloon, but most of them were exported.

MkV would have been a show-stopper in its own right, but Lyons had something more impressive up his sleeve, and this, of course, was the XK 120. The bronze roadster on its turntable at Earls Court was something quite new: far more revolutionary than the first SS.I or the original 2½-litre Jaguar saloon.

Consider the specification by the standards of 1948: a habitable aerodynamic two-seater on a modern, independently-sprung chassis, powered by a twin overhead camshaft engine developing 160bhp (the same as the latest in 5.4-litre overhead-valve Cadillacs from Detroit). A top speed estimated at 120mph added up to the sort of thing that a Continental maker might have attempted, at £2,000, way back in 1939. But £2,000 pre-war meant something like £3,750 in the Stafford Cripps era, and this was not William Lyons' idea at all. The XK 120 listed at

Only Jaguar can make a Jaguar, as this Belgian coachbuilder found out when he attempted a Ferrari shape in 1951

£1,275, inclusive of British purchase tax.

Until then even a single overhead camshaft was considered too noisy for the general public, only Singer remaining loyal to this configuration after Lord Nuffield's wholesale abandonment of ohc in 1936. As for two overhead camshafts, these were considered beyond the laity, and also beyond the ordinary garage. Such engines had been found on the Type 57 Bugatti and the Alfa-Romeo; the hottest of Ettore's Type 57s gave 200bhp and 125-130mph, and the Alfa could match such performance with the aid of twin blowers. One did not, however, use such machinery for shopping, and production was minimal: only thirty '2.9' Alfas were sold, and not many more 57S and 57SC Bugattis. Aerodynamic sports bodies, of course, were no novelty. If the hand-

some FIATs and Lancias used in the last pre-war Mille Miglia had been made in penny numbers, there was always the successful and frequently-encountered Type-328 BMW. The XK's great significance was that it modified the concept of the sports car as generally understood.

What is a sports car, anyway? No more than a vehicle intended to be driven for sheer enjoyment, and in pre-XK days one accepted certain penalties as part of the fun. These included hard suspension, too many decibels, vibration, a gear change and clutch which demanded considerable skill, over-geared steering, a finicky appetite for fuel and spark plugs alike and, in the case of women drivers, controls which left the unfortunate conductress the choice of keeping her feet on the pedals or her hindquarters on the seat. All-weather equipment was considered effete: either it did not protect at all, or it assumed the status of an aircraft's blind-flying hood. To erect what the manufacturer provided involved the

crew in a nightmare game with sticks and pieces of canvas. By contrast the XK 120 was quiet, softly suspended, blessed with almost too-easy synchromesh (the 'crash' bottom gear had yet to provoke strictures), and light enough on the hands for any woman. The engine was sufficiently untemperamental even for the miserable 'Pool' petrol of the era, and the ample mudguarding kept the elements out. If the hood impeded rearward vision, it was at least weathertight.

It was also as reliable as its simpler forebears. Accessibility was never the Jaguar's strong suit, but six-figure mileages between overhauls were not uncommon. Further, the new engine

The classic, uncluttered shape of the 1956 twin-cam Jaguar engine

remained the company's staple for more than twenty years, powering all manner of saloons from the compact 2.4-litre to the vast MkX family, as well as being applied to out and-out competition machinery – the C- and D-types which put on 'the fastest scheduled service possible' at Le Mans, other sports-racers by Cooper, HWM, and Lister, and even Norman Buckley's record-breaking speedboats. By early 1966 a quarter of a million twin-cam Jaguar sixes had been turned out. The late Ron Flockhart, who drove Ecurie Ecosse's D-types to such good purpose, likened it to the Rolls-Royce Merlin: 'it felt as if it would go on for ever'. If 265bhp has so far been the limit for touring units, some of the fiercer racing versions have exceeded the 300 mark.

The XK's genesis goes back to the war years, when Lyons, Heynes and Baily were fire-watching. Initially the engine was conceived as a power unit for the saloons, the sports two-seater which would not call for constant revision of design to keep abreast of competition'.

Initially, of course, Jaguar hedged their bets by evolving two parallel models – an economy type to circumvent the British horsepower tax (and of course the capacity tax which succeeded it in 1947), and something bigger for export customers. An es-

Leslie Johnson wins the Production Car Race at Silverstone, August 1949, in his racing debut

being merely a test-bed. Once again Harry Weslake supervised head design, and Heynes later summarised the team's primary objective as 'to produce a series of engines with a higher basic performance than is normally possible, sential prerequisite was a high degree of parts interchangeability between the two types. Vee-eights and vee-twelves were considered, but tradition dies hard, and it was finally decided to use in-line units – a four and a six. From the beginning relatively long strokes were favoured: only twice have Jaguar deviated from this pattern, with the 83 x 76.5mm 2.4-litre made from 1956 to 1968, and on the 2.8-litre version of the XJ 6 which succeeded it.

The first X (for experimental) engine of the new series was running soon after the war. This 1,360cc 4-cylinder XF had many similarities with the XK as we know it, especially in head design, but the crankshaft could not cope with the high revs demanded, so recourse was had to a 1.8-litre development

with cross push-rods as in BMW (Type-XG). Noisy valve gear eliminated this development which gave way in its turn to the 2-litre XJ, once again a twin ohc motor. One of these was loaned to Colonel Gardner for use in his record-breaking MG. Alongside this was evolved a 3.2-litre six, also designated XJ (no connection with the familiar 1968 theme). A lack of low-speed torque was

the trouble, but lengthening the piston stroke from 98mm to 106mm solved the final problem.

Features of the 6-cylinder engine as unveiled in 1948 were a massive seven-bearing crankshaft forged from sixty-five-ton steel, and an alloy head weighing a mere fifty pounds. Weslake had done his work well. The valves were set at seventy degrees to the vertical, and the twin camshafts were chain-driven. Hemispherical combustion chambers not only conferred extra efficiency and a better flow of cooling water to the valve seats; they were also simpler to machine. Conventional wet-sump lubrication was always used on the touring engines, 12-volt coil ignition and twin horizontal SU carburetters completed the underbonnet specification, and output of the 6-cylinder XK was 160 bhp at 5,000rpm. Production cylinder blocks were, incidentally, made for Jaguar by Leyland, an interesting anticipation of the merger which created the British Leyland Motor Corporation in 1967.

Most of the preliminary road tests were undertaken on the six, for the 4-cylinder XK 100 was a 'car that never was'. It would have been an attractive proposition with 50bhp per litre, and it figured in Jaguar's 1949 and 1950 catalogues, but the only 4-cylinder prototype to take the road was a special affair with air-strut suspension, and the 3.4-litre model's success caused the abandonment of the programme. It is untrue that, as has been asserted, a twin-cam 4-cylinder engine was originally envisaged for the 2.4-litre saloon, as work on this did not begin until four years after the conclusion of work on the XJ.

An outstanding engine was one thing, but the Jaguar team had produced an outstanding chassis to match it. The box-section frame with its box-section cross-members offered great torsional rigidity, while the suspension resembled that of Mk V, with torsion bars at the front and conventional semi-elliptics at the rear. The XK's hydraulic brakes were, however, of

Appleyard's Alpine. The legendary NUB 120 halts in company with one of its rivals, the stark J2 Allard

Lockheed rather than Girling type, and the handbrake lever was a fly-off affair on the floor. The gearbox had well-spaced ratios (3.64, 4.98, 7.22 and 12.29 to 1) and there was synchromesh on top, third and second. The aerodynamic body had all the functional elegance that the public had come to expect of William Lyons, and a narrow oval grille replaced the classic radiator. Only the top of the bonnet opened, alligator-fashion. A vee screen was standard equipment, the rear wheels were concealed behind detachable spats, and there was a surprising amount of room for baggage in the sloping tail.

Inevitably scoffers dismissed this latest Jaguar as a 'come-on' to attract customers to MkV; if it ever reached the public, they said, it would either be impossibly expensive or disappointing-ly slow. Not that the British public stood much chance of ever getting an XK 120: eighty per cent of the 1949 output was already earmarked for dollar customers, and Jaguar's New York agents asserted that they had taken ninety orders on the strength of the brochure alone. In the end, only about eight per cent of all XK 120s built stayed in Britain, and the model took quite a while to get into production, American deliveries starting in July 1949. None were sold at home before March 1950.

Before this, however, the XK had shown that it was no promenade car. In May 1949, R M V Sutton, who had been responsible for development testing, took a standard model to Jabbeke and covered a flying mile under official observation at 132.596

Norman Dewis's 1953 Jabbeke car is a little stark, and the cockpit cover suggests the Space Age, but this XK 120 was very nearly stock

mph. It ran with the optional under-shield and 3.27:1 axle ratio, and also without hood or screen, but even in full road trim the speed still exceeded 126mph. To clinch this performance, a team of three XKs in red, white and blue respectively, turned out for the Production Car Race at Silverstone, which they proceeded to dominate, Leslie Johnson winning at 82.8mph with Peter Walker in second place. A standard model tested by *The Motor* recorded 125mph on top, 90 on third, and 62 on second, as well as taking only 6.7 seconds to go from 10-30mph in top gear. Using all ratios, of course, the getaway was electrifying: 0-30mph in 3.2 seconds, and 0-60 in ten seconds. Fuel consumptions of the order of 18-20mpg were possible, the car could be started in second gear, and the only serious faults were fade-prone brakes and headlamps which restricted safe cruising at night to around 70mph. If the suspension was soft by sports-car standards, directional ability was little impaired.

Racing started in earnest in 1950, when the model chalked up a class win at Silverstone, not to mention one for Phil Hill in California's Pebble Beach Cup. More important, Stirling Moss and Peter Walker took first and second places in the revived Tourist Trophy at Dundrod, which was some compensation for retirements in the Targa Florio and at Le Mans. Johnson was fifth in the Mille Miglia. The season also saw the first appearance of a famous combination – Ian Appleyard and the white XK 120, NUB 120. Together they made the best individual performance in that favourite Jaguar stamping-ground, the 'Alpine', collecting a *Coupe des Alpes* and the class honours as well. Though the touring XK never matched the racing record of the

A wide range of options was available by 1955. The XK 140 drophead coupé has the standard disc wheels, and the occasional-four fixed-head coupé is seen here with wire wheels. The quest for spaciousness is reflected in the more bulbous lines of the 1957 XK 150 fixed-head coupé

specialized C- and D-types, it had a long and distinguished career in front of it, and this did not end until 1960, when Haddon and Vivian won their class in the 'Tulip' with an XK 150.

The new sports car might be but a stepping stone to a new generation of saloons, but by 1950 Jaguar were making 250 cars a week, and more

RJ Adams motors smartly round Cadwell in his XK 140 roadster, one of the few released to the home market

space was urgently needed. This was found well out of town at Allesley, where the firm took over the former Number 2 Daimler Shadow Factory, a relic of the frantic re-armament programme of 1938. Since the war it had been used for car and bus production, but it was too big for Daimler. Jaguar were only too grateful to have a million square feet of floor space under their control. The move from Foleshill was complete by 1952.

Interesting exploits continued. With the arrival of the C-type in 1951 the XK 120's role was transferred to club racing and rallies, but it proved itself a tough road car as well. A Mr Leslie Taylor set up an interesting record in 1951, when he drove the 965 miles from Darwin to Alice Springs (Australia) at an average of 91mph, lopping five-and-a-half hours off the previous best time down 'The Bitumen'. The police did not approve, and booked him on three charges! In 1954 a Señor Lucio Bollaert successfully crossed the Andes on another XK 120; on this occasion bad roads were less of a handicap than Chilean pump fuel, allegedly 76 octane but actually rather worse.

The XK 120 range had been further

widened, a fixed-head coupé joining the range in March 1951, and a drophead late in 1953. 1952 saw the arrival of 'special equipment' models distinguishable by their 180bhp engines with high-lift camshafts, lightened flywheels, twin exhausts and centre-lock wire wheels in place of the standard type's discs. One of the coupés gave an impressive demonstration of speed and reliability at Paris's Montlhéry Autodrome. In seven days and seven nights a formidable team of drivers – Stirling Moss, Leslie Johnson, Bert Hadley and Jack Fairman – covered 16,852 miles at a speed of 100.31mph. An engine strip-down at the end revealed that the crankshaft was still within production tolerances. Over short distances the XK could go even faster. In the spring of 1953 Norman Dewis recorded 141.846mph at Jabbeke, and a staggering 172.412mph over the same course in October. Admittedly on this latter occasion the car wore a cockpit hood and 'full optional equipment', but it ran on pump fuel imported from England. It is amusing to note that Dewis's second attempt took place a few days after one of the exotic 2.8-litre supercharged vee-

1958 XK 150 drophead coupé undergoes 'the water torture'. Its new grille shows similarities to the 2.4-litre and 3.4-litre saloons

Export-only XK 150 roadster with left-hand drive and whitewalls, 1958

eight Pegasos from Spain had done 151mph on the Belgian motorway. Nobody would have remarked, as had William Boddy of an early production XK 120 that Wilfredo Ricart's complex masterpiece was 'like a bank clerk, quite devoid of temperament!'

Also in 1953 America voted the four-year-old XK 120 'the No 1 sports car of the year', while Sherwood Johnston won the national sports-car driver's championship, and it was now possible to buy a new roadster for the equivalent of £1,193 – nearly £250 off the old price, and a good £400 less than was asked of the few Britons fortunate enough to get one. Back at the factory, of course, the XK was now playing second fiddle to the MkVII saloon introduced for 1951. Statistics tell their own story: only 20,992 XK 120s and 140s between 1949 and 1957, as against nearly 31,000 MkVIIs in an appreciably shorter period. From 1956 onwards, of course, the company was also turning out another closed model, the 2.4-litre.

The XK theme, of course, was far from finished, even if it had been outgunned (or, more strictly, outbraked) on

the circuits. Disc brakes, first tried on a C-type in the 1952 Mille Miglia, were not to reach the touring range until 1957, but the XK140 of 1955 incorporated not a few of the lessons learned on sports-racers and saloons alike.

For the latest model, an improved version of the 'special equipment' engine with high-lift camshafts and oil-insulated coil was standardized, output rising to 190bhp. Special Equipment XK 140s were even more powerful, with 210bhp C-type units, hence the designation 'XK 140MC' used in America. These variants also had wire wheels and twin exhausts, while other legacies from the racing programme were the superb rack-and-pinion steering, which replaced the recirculating ball type found on the XK 120, and a discreet little medallion on the boot lid commemorating two victories at Le Mans – three more such triumphs were to be added to the score before the last of the XK family gave way to the unitary-construction E-type in 1961. From Mk VII came the option of overdrive on top gear, though Jaguar's third regular option, Borg-Warner automatic, did not reach the sports-car range until the latter part of 1956. Only 827 automatic XK 140s were made.

Mechanically the XK 140 marked a signal improvement, and independent road tests revealed that it was fractionally faster, at 129mph, than Mercedes-Benz's fabulous 300SL gull-wing coupé, though the German car was some two seconds quicker to 60mph, and not much thirstier thanks to its fuel-injection engine. But superb though the Mercedes was, it was tricky to drive and expensive to maintain; it cost £4,393 in England at a time when the Jaguar could still be bought for less than £2,000; and it was made in far smaller quantities; 1,400 between 1954 and 1956. The provision of two rear seats for children, however, rather spoilt the lines of the new XK coupés, though the roadster's flawless shape remained untouched, apart from a rather fussy new grille.

The summer of 1957 saw the last of the line, the XK 150. Here was unashamed bulboid which disappointed even the most fervid admirers of the Lyons line, though a wider bonnet made for easier access to the internals, and the back seats were now usable over short distances, making the car almost a GT. Alas, only coupés were offered; the roadster was dropped.

A closer look, however, revealed that here was a fine car indeed. Engine and transmission options were inherited from the 140, but though disc wheels were still standard equipment, almost every XK 150 wore the wire type used on Special Equipment versions. These latter also possessed an entirely new departure, Dunlop disc brakes on all four wheels. Jaguar never adopted the disc/drum combination favoured by many other makers, and a preproduction car had proved its mettle by undertaking thirty consecutive stops from 100mph with only a minute's pause between each. Prices ranged from £1,764 up to £2,161 for a Special Equipment drophead coupé with automatic. A similar overdrive-equipped car came up for test during the year: it weighed in at 28¾ cwt., and proved capable of 124mph. The 0-30mph acceleration time was down to 2.8 seconds, and the 60 mark came up in 8½ seconds. The brakes were rated as near perfect as possible, being innocent of fade and judder alike, while the new long-range beam headlamps allowed of safe cruising speeds of up to 100mph. By contrast, the luggage boot was considered less than adequate.

During 1958 the roadster reappeared, though prices were quoted only in dollars – $4,495 for the 'Special' with 210bhp engine, and $5,090 when fitted with Jaguar's latest high-performance unit, the 'Gold Top' with a new Weslake-designed straight-port head and three SU carburetters. In this guise 250bhp were available, and the new XK150S variant was supplied only with disc brakes and overdrive. S-types reached the home market in 1959, by which time they could be had with the firm's largest and most powerful engine to date, the 3.8-litre developing 265bhp. Also new was the Powr-Lok limited-slip differential. One of these S-types was tried by *The Motor*, its 132mph top speed making it the fastest closed car ever to be tested by that journal. A 0-100mph time of 20.3 seconds, a standing quarter-mile in 16.2 seconds, and better than 25mpg at a constant 70mph added up to a remarkable £2,187-worth of motor-car.

But the writing was on the wall. There were no XKs of any sort on the Jaguar stand at Earls Court in 1959 or 1960, and when I visited the Jaguar works in February 1961, there were none to be seen in the despatch bay, either. What many people consider to be 'the last of the real Jaguars' was on its way out. It had won many friends: even Cecil Clutton, a former President of the Vintage Sports Car Club, described his 150 as 'a really splendid motor car' and in 1971, a decade after the last one left Coventry, good examples can still command around £900 ($2,250).

The 1961 Geneva Show was, of course, to mark the debut of a new type of sporting Jaguar, the legendary E-type. Americans persist in calling it the XK-E. But it is not the same thing.

CARRIAGES AND COMPACTS

Among those who bought Mk VIIs in 1952 was 'Goldie' Gardner, who had used a prototype twin–cam Jaguar engine in the 1948 version of his MG Streamliner

The XK 120 was a revolution to Europeans and Americans alike: but to William Lyons and his team it was but a stepping-stone to a high-performance saloon which was finally to obliterate the 'Wardour Street Bentley' image of the 1930s. These two, parallel, lines of development were to earn their creator two signal honours – that of a Royal Designer for Industry (the first to be accorded to anyone in the automobile world) in 1954, and a knighthood in 1956.

Again, however, it was not what was done that mattered; it was how Jaguar did it. Big, luxurious sporting saloons had long been a British forte, especially in the 1930s. Then the Rolls-Royce-

built Bentley really had been a 'Silent Sports Car', even if it disliked sustained high revs. It was ably backed by Smith-Clarke's 6-cylinder Alvises and by a new generation of Lagondas from the drawing-board of W O Bentley. These latter had culminated in a splendid $4\frac{1}{2}$-litre vee-twelve, the first catalogued saloon to put a hundred miles into the hour, and backed by handling which still measured up to the standards of the mid-1950s, a remarkable feat for a bulky two-tonner. The Lagonda's failings were complexity (it was difficult to service), thirst (12-14mpg), and a high price. Even in 1939 it could not comfortably be marketed at less than £1,500, and thus had priced itself right out of the picture in the Cripps era. Bentley later regretted his decision to abandon development in 1945, but subsequent developments have shown how right he was.

The original XK programme had shown Jaguar's foresight, and already Lyons was looking ahead at the American scene. The pushrod models had sold as Old English Traditional, but for all their excellent performance they could match the native product only on well-surfaced roads. Their hard suspension and low ground clearance meant a terrific hammering on the dusty by-roads of the West, and handsome though the unadorned single-blade bumpers were, they were by no means proof against United States parking habits, backed by the national wear in heavily-chromed overriders. Even in overall performance the big Jaguar, on 125bhp, could only just match the speed of Detroit's bigger eights, and this before Oldsmobile set a new trend in 1949 with their advanced ohv Rocket. 70-plus on third meant nothing to Americans who detested shifting anyway (automatic transmission had been around since 1940), while

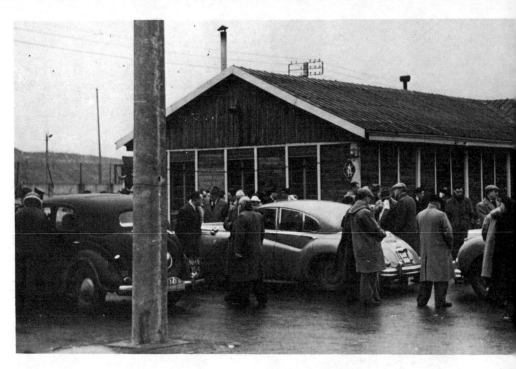

British 'sports sedans' were cramped five-seaters with inadequate baggage accommodation for a long vacation trip to Mexico or Canada. Thus William Lyons became Europe's first successful exponent of a mid-Atlantic idiom.

His 3½-litre MkVII unveiled at Earls Court in 1950 was a full five-six seater with luggage room to match. Its streamlining was not aggressive enough to offend (like the unfortunate A90 Austin of 1948); yet contemporary enough in style to avoid comparison with the already-fancied classics of the 1930s. It possessed the sort of brute horsepower that appealed to Americans. Today, when off-the-peg Cadillacs run to eight litres plus and 400bhp, the 250-odd horses of a Jaguar seem small beer, but consider the line-up in 1951, the MkVII's first season. Top of that year's Big League in Detroit were the ohv Cadillac and Chrysler's new hemi-head vee-eight, both 5½-litre units. Cadillac offered 160bhp, and Chrysler twenty more. An average example of either turned the scales at about two tons, and though the Chrysler was good for an easy 100mph, both Detroit offerings were 'an awful lot of auto-

mobile'. On the credit side their fully automatic transmissions rendered them admirable long-range transport providing the brakes were treated with respect, American vee-eights made up for fearsome maintenance costs with almost proverbial reliability, and the list price of a Chrysler Imperial was £1,275 at par.

The Jaguar was nearly as roomy, appreciably lighter, and its 160bhp could match the Chrysler's speed. It could also out-accelerate America's best up to 60mph, though as automatics grew more sophisticated this lead was not maintained. Its handling was streets ahead, and even in the drum-brake era (Chrysler's pioneer use of discs was short-lived) Britain's hydraulics were superior to America's. Nor was it much more expensive, at $3,850 (about £1,400). In passing, it is fair to say that the sporting generation of American cars spearheaded by the Ford Mustang of 1964 were inspired by the Jaguar.

Obviously, however, no foreign import could make a sizeable hole in Detroit's vast annual sales of automobiles. Dealer-coverage would never

66

sensational, and the extent of its impact is shown in the diversity of owners, VIP customers ranging from Her Majesty Queen Elizabeth The Queen Mother to Alberto Ascari. The engine was standard XK, set five inches further forward in a frame which closely resembled that of the sports model. Also an XK heritage was the four-speed synchromesh gearbox with its stubby and delightfully positive central change. The immense baggage capacity was obtained by mounting the twin fuel tanks in the rear wings. The slab-sided bodywork possessed a definite wing-line, and the wide radiator grille had affinities with the old MkV, which was continued for a further season. The trim was traditional British, with real leather upholstery, interior woodwork and a sliding roof. The 'Prima Ballerina of the London Show' measured $184\frac{1}{2}$ inches from stem to stern, and of course it was reserved for export.

American reaction was predictable, to the tune of $27 million worth of orders in the first few months. The new Allesley factory was fast becoming essential, especially as the advent of MkVII coincided with Jaguar's first win at Le Mans in 1951. The firm's percentage of exports shot up to a record ninety-six per cent, unsurpassed before or since.

With all this performance available, there was no immediate need to join in the horsepower race, though this was reaching interesting proportions on the other side of the Atlantic. The first C-type Jaguar sports-racers of 1951 had 210 brake horses under their bonnets: 1953 Cadillacs could match this, while by this time five other American makers had bettered the XK unit's 160bhp. But in order to stay competitive an automatic option was essential, and early in 1953 Lyons followed Rolls-Royce's lead by offering the two-speed Borg-Warner transmission on MkVIIs for the US market. The only automatic

match that of GM or Chrysler, and the vast majority of Americans did not want William Lyons' way of being different. But for the first time a British maker had produced a car that the US market could take seriously, and when the MkVII was withdrawn in 1957, it had scored up not only Jaguar's longest run to date, but also record sales for any SS or Jaguar type. It is also interesting to compare MkVII's record with that of its closest European rival, the single-cam Mercedes-Benz 300. Thanks to their inexpensive and frugal 4-cylinder diesels, Stuttgart have always had the overall edge on Coventry, but the original 300 shape, which survived for ten years until 1961, accounted for a mere 11,430 units.

MkVII is now outmoded. It is too big for congested roads (I sold my MkVIII in 1958 because it could not cope with London traffic and bought a 3.4 saloon instead); the small window area makes it look ponderous beside latter-day XJs; and figures like 102mph over the quarter-mile and 0-60mph in 14.7 seconds are within the compass of any so-called GT saloon in the $1\frac{1}{2}$-litre class. By the standards of 1951, however, it was

cars released for England before the end of 1955 were a batch supplied to the Victor Britain rental firm, but for dollar customers only. In 1954 MkVII became available with another option, electrically-selected overdrive on top gear, and this was soon to become a favourite with Britons. (Since then, incidentally, Jaguar saloon customers have always had three choices of gearbox, despite the spread of compulsory automatic on other rival makes). Some of the early overdrives were apt to be jerky on upward and downward changes, but the step-up in ratio (from 4.27 to 3.54:1 on the MkVII) made for quiet and effortless cruising, not to mention an overall 20mpg

MkVII also proved a surprisingly good rally car, Cotton and Herteaux taking fourth and sixth places respectively in the 1952 'Monte' while Ian and Pat Appleyard were second in the Tulip. Subsequent 'Montes' upheld the tradition: second for the Appleyards in 1953, a 6th and an 8th in 1954, the

Charles Faroux Team Trophy in 1955, and finally, in 1956, an outright victory for the Belfast pair, Adams and Biggar. If MkVII's only other big win was that of Parsons and Mrs Vann in the 1954 Round Britain event, there were several class triumphs to add to the score.

More important, the big cars spearheaded Jaguar's penetration of a new sport that was to reach the headlines in 1958, saloon-car racing. In those early days the machines which took part really were 'stock', and the MkVIIs had little serious opposition. Their first appearance was at the International Trophy Meeting at Silverstone in May 1952, when Stirling Moss scored a double, beating a Healey and an Allard at 75.22mph, as well as collecting the honours for big production sports cars on a C-type. He did it again with a Mk VII in 1953, though beaten by Apple-

yard and Rolt in 1954, while in the 1955 race Mike Hawthorn was the victor, at nearly 79mph. The 1956 winner, Ivor Bueb, was hard pressed by Duncan Hamilton in one of the new compact 2.4-litres, and a year later the ferocious '3.4' had taken over. The king-size Jaguars never raced again. They had, in any case, been less fortunate in long-distance events: the Mille Miglia had seen the MkVIIs outpaced by Paul Frère's enormous Chrysler, and they were never allowed to avenge an indifferent showing in the 1951 Carrera Panamericana, since the organisers subsequently banned twin-carburetter engines in the touring category.

190bhp engines came with the MkVIIM of 1955, which also boasted closer gear ratios and reinforced suspension. By the end of the year home buyers had the choice of all three transmission options, though Americans got automatic unless they specified manual. Semaphore-type direction indicators gave way to flashers. 1956 automatic Jaguars incorporated an intermediate hold engaged by a 'kickdown' linked to the accelerator pedal. In this additional ratio 72mph was

The 1952 'Monte'. Left: One of the French-entered Mk VIIs which finished well up the list. Below: B E Bradnack's somewhat battered specimen at a control; the extra armoury of horns was evidently of no avail

available, and the higher degree of driver-control made many converts to the American style of painless shifting.

Even better was the MkVIII of 1957, which kept pace with the sports-car programme by using the 210bhp engine. A revised grille and a single-piece curved screen in place of MkVII's divided-type improved the appearance, while none of the luxury was lost. For

ment. Nor did the Suez crisis and its attendant fuel rationing upset Jaguar as much as might have been expected: it merely enabled them to catch up with a formidable backlog of home orders.

This brief respite was more than counterbalanced, however, by the disastrous fire of February 1957, which did damage estimated at £3½ million and wrote off well over 200 cars

Intermediate model. The 1957 Mk VIII saloon anticipated the definitive Mk IX of 1959, though it retained the 3.4–litre engine

one's £1,830 (admittedly £550 more than was asked for the first MkVIIs) one got a heater, folding tables, an electric clock, three cigar lighters, pile carpets and a nylon rug in the rear compart-

awaiting despatch. It also killed the D-type's road-going sister, the XK-SS, as among the other casualties were this model's body panels and jigs.

MkVIII did not last long, for some 6,000 only were made in a couple of seasons. The 1958 London Show saw MkIX, the last Jaguar to have a separate chassis frame. It was also the first touring Jaguar to use the 3.8-litre engine introduced on the 1957 racing D-types, the first model to fit disc brakes as standard equipment, and the first-ever Jaguar to be listed with power-assisted steering, which meant only 3½ turns from lock to lock, as against 4¾ for the original MkVII. Even in detuned form the big unit gave 220bhp, but maximum speed was up to 113mph: Jaguar were entering the 'motorway era' with a

vehicle which could cruise comfortably at 100mph. The costliest version with automatic transmission sold for £2,163. MkIX's worst fault was a heavy thirst, but it was a splendid carriage for executives. The descendants of the Wardour Street Bentleys were becoming ambassadorial wear. The Nigerian government ordered forty MkIXs finished in the national colours of green and white, and when President de Gaulle paid a state visit to Canada in 1960, he motored in a big Jaguar rather than in the traditional Cadillac or Lincoln associated with trans-Atlantic motorcades. It was not lost on the motoring public that the factory slogan of the early 1950s, 'Grace, Space, Pace', had given way to 'A Special Kind of Motoring That No Other Car in The World Can Offer'. MkIX's last year was 1961: its successor was destined to be yet another show-stopper in the best Lyons manner, but it belonged to a new generation.

The E-type is generally regarded as the first of the modern Jaguars, but the present era at Allesley can be traced back to 1956, and the birth of the compact models. The 2.4-litre unveiled at Earls Court in the autumn of 1955 is the true ancestor of a series that has come to spell 'Jaguar' to the world by extending the scope of Jaguar-ownership to a far wider income group. The family's thirteen-year run saw some 200,000 cars delivered, of which all but about 31,000 were MkIIs of one kind and another. Their influence was widespread, and they sparked off such important developments as the purchase of Daimler in May 1960, and assembly of completely-knocked-down units in South Africa a few months later. They were a complete vindication of Lyons' perfect shape, and Heynes' concept of an engine good for many years of steady development, for to the end of their days they remained twin-cam sixes, and the outline was little altered. They were the firm's best all-rounders, performing with distinction in rallies and saloon-car races alike. With them Jaguar waged a successful price-war in an era of galloping inflation. A 2.4-litre saloon with manual four-speed gearbox listed at £1,344 in 1956: its 1967 descendant, called a 240, had more power, all-round disc brakes and a synchronised bottom gear, in spite of which it cost a mere £21 more. No wonder these first unitary-construction models pushed Jaguar firmly into the Big League. Before 1956, annual production had only twice exceeded the 10,000 mark, in 1953 and 1954: thereafter, not even the fire could produce a serious recession, and 1959 was Jaguar's first 20,000 year.

By mid-1955 everyone knew there was to be a new Jaguar model. Some people thought that the old XK 100 4-cylinder might be revived, but fours were no longer acceptable in this market, as Armstrong Siddeley discovered to their cost when they sought to challenge the 2.4-litre with their 234. It handled better than the early compact Jaguar but its ugliness was not its only handicap. The vee-eight canard also reared its head; this rumour was traced back to a proto-type 9-litre ohc tank engine which was under development at the time, but dropped as a result of the defence cuts of 1958.

Instead, of course, Heynes adhered

The compact shape. In early days the rear quarters were a little blind, but the 1959 3.4-litre still looks good today

A 2.4-litre at the 1956 International Trophy Meeting. Silverstone was for many years a successful ground for the big closed Jaguars

to the faithful six, unchanged in concept, but with the piston stroke drastically shortened to reduce the capacity from 3.4-litres to 2,483cc. Such a unit had in fact been tried in one of the 1954 TT D-types, but only to take advantage of a race formula which favoured smaller engines. At 112bhp, the 2.4-litre's output roughly matched that of Riley's classic long-stroke four, now nearing the end of a long run: it was, however, well ahead of anything offered by family-car makers such as Austin, Ford and Vauxhall, who were still content with less than 90bhp.

The rest of it was a revolution. The wheel had come full circle, and a firm which had started as body-builders now procured their unitary hulls, complete if 'in the white', from Pressed Steel of Oxford. Front suspension was by coils and wishbones, where the XKs and

MkVIIs used torsion bars. Equally novel was the trailing-link rear suspension with cantilever springs, insulated with rubber blocks which eliminated the irritating drumming noises associated with unitary construction. The Lockheed Brake-master hydraulic brakes were servo-assisted, and special equipment models came with heaters, clocks, and Jaguar mascots. Overdrive was optional from the start, but automatic 2.4s did not appear until 1958.

Like all entirely new designs, the 2.4-litre had its faults. Testers disliked the cranked gear lever, and the servo brakes, in the manner of their kind, demanded too much thinking-time in traffic. The suspension was rather too supple, though even the sterner critics admitted that it furnished an admirable compromise between independence at

Showing its tail to the opposition, a 3.8-litre automatic in the winter of 1962 reveals the styling differences of the later type

the rear and an orthodox beam axle. Like all twin-cam Jaguars, however, this was a 100mph car, the short-stroke engine thrived on high revs, and it was the most frugal Jaguar since the demise of the 2½-litre MkV in 1951. Some owners spoke of 25-28mpg. No wonder nearly 20,000 enthusiasts chose the original 2.4.

The model was seldom raced or rallied: the 3.4-litre came too soon to give it a chance. Nonetheless, it had its brief moment of glory in 1956, when Paul Frère won the Belgian Production Touring-Car Race at 96.64mph on a very special, works-prepared example with large-bore SU carburetters, a C-type head, and a close-ratio box. This one, incidentally, was a nightmare for the pit staff at Spa: they found out the hard way what happens when one tries to extract the box from a unit-construction saloon without also removing the engine!

The factory fire in 1957, of course, coincided with an entirely logical development, the 3.4-litre. On the

A 3.8-litre Mk II saloon of the early 1960s gets away from the start at Brunton Hill-Climb

surface this was just a marriage of the 2.4-litre hull to the 210bhp version of the bigger engine, with cutaway rear-wheel spats and a new grille to remind other drivers that they were taking on something special. Underneath, there was quite a lot of extra engineering: an enlarged radiator block, stiffer engine bearers, and reinforced suspension. But if the 2.4-litre was a fast car, its big sister was a bomb. Top speed was up by 19mph to 120mph, and manual-gearbox versions could almost reach 100mph in third. Even when automatic was specified, the 3.4 reached 60mph 3.4 seconds before a manual 2.4-litre, while the measure of progress (and the influence of racing) can best be gauged by the 3.4's 0-100mph time of twenty-six seconds: more than two seconds faster than a special equipment XK 120 tested in 1952. A top speed of 80mph in intermediate helped to cancel out the previous snags of automatic Jaguars. Handling, admittedly, was rather untidy on corners, and owners like myself who drove their cars fast and far were left with the uneasy feeling that the 3.4 might play an alarming trick or two. In my case, the replacement of the original tyres by Dunlop Durabands helped the situation, though it did not altogether cure it. But the 3.4 was just what America wanted; already the move towards the compacts of 1960 was on the way, and by 1957 the MkVIII was considered too big, and the 2.4-litre 'underpowered'. It was not, of course, but such a reaction was logical at a time when even the basic Chevrolet Six claimed 140bhp, though it was never stated how much of this reached the back wheels!

1958 models of the compact Jaguars were available with wire wheels and Dunlop disc brakes all round, ninety-five per cent of customers specifying the latter: already *The Autocar* considered that it was 'false economy' to rely on drums with anything so potent

75

as the 3.4-litre, and certainly the press finally stopped criticising Jaguar brakes. The 3.4-litre was also making its mark in rallies, while its first appearance in quantity on British roads coincided with a sharp upswing in the popularity of saloon-car racing and the establishment of a British Championship. The curtain on this new era was rung up, appropriately, by Mike Hawthorn's victory at Silverstone in September 1957, when he averaged an impressive 82.19mph. In 1958, Jaguar profits passed £1,000,000 for the first time, and at the 1959 Show the firm launched the definitive MkII series. With them came a range of options verging on infinity, plus the elimination of all the bugs encountered on the so-called MkI models.

Jaguar had already sunk £1,000,000 into tooling for unitary construction, and they were determined to have their money's worth. Front suspension with a higher roll centre and a wider track at the rear dealt with the handling troubles. Disc brakes were standard, and the wrap-round rear window gave vastly superior all-round vision. A restyled instrument panel made for greater convenience and safety, and fog lamps were fitted to all cars for the home market. The 3.4-litre engines were unchanged, but improvements in cylinder-head design boosted the 2.4's output to 120bhp. There was also a new and fiercer model using the 220bhp 3.8-litre engine developed for MkIX and on these a limited-slip differential formed part of the package. The result was a 'dual-personality' car, capable of 125mph but willing to run happily up to 6,000rpm on the indirect gears like any member of the new GT generation. A fleet of 3.8s equipped the first police unit to operate on the M1 motorway.

Nor was the MkII theme worked out. There was a new variation in the 1963 catalogue, though this time it called itself a Daimler, used that company's 2½-litre Turner-designed vee-eight engine, and was initially sold only with automatic gearbox. The last major

improvement to the MkII range came in 1966, when a synchromesh bottom gear was provided. 1967 saw price cuts, financed by the deletion of the fog lamps and some austerities in the trim. Only the 2.4-litre, renamed the 240, survived a rationalisation which followed the British Leyland merger. The end of the line came during 1969.

By this time, of course, the Jaguar compacts were no longer seen on the circuits, but their career reached its zenith at the beginning of the 1960s. The 3.4-litre had dominated saloon-car racing in 1958 and 1959, and in 1960, when the 3.8-litre had taken over, Jack Sears won the British Saloon Car Championship on one of T E B Sopwith's cars. Among those who won for Jaguar were Graham Hill, Roy Salvadori, and even, on one occasion in 1960, Colin Chapman of Lotus fame, who later bought a MkII for his own use : he was not the only 'outside' manufacturer to do so. 1961 and 1962 were also Jaguar years, but during the latter season the big American Chevrolets twice gave the MkIIs some close competition. 1963 was the turning-point, as the Ford Galaxies moved in. There were defeats at Silverstone's International Trophy Meeting at Aintree, and at the Crystal Palace. On a miserable July day the Salmon/Sutcliffe 3.8-litre successfully fought off Sir Gawaine Baillie's very fast Ford to win *The Motor*'s Six-Hour Saloon Car Race at Brands.Hatch. It was subsequently disqualified, but other Jaguars were awarded first and second places – the 3.8's competition swansong in Britain.

Big cars could still win rallies, as the days of the SAAB, the Mini and the Escort were yet to come, and the 3.4-litre of Morley and Hercock won the 1959 Tulip. In the 1960 Alpine Jaguars won their class and two *Coupés des Alpes,* while Bernard Consten collected the touring category of the Tour de France. He did it again in 1962 and 1963 though, as in England, the Fords of Detroit moved in for the 1964 competition.

There were other laurels. A jump of

fifty per cent in West German Jaguar sales during 1963 had quite a lot to do with the exploits of the German concessionaire, Peter Lindner, who won that year's Six-Hour Touring Car Race at the Nürburgring in direct competition with the Mercedes-Benz works team. He also performed with distinction at Brands Hatch, while his regular co-driver Peter Nocker was the winner of the 1963 European Touring Car Challenge. But perhaps the high spot of 1963, ironically the last year in which a

their 1959 show report, 'for the sports cars they didn't see fit to display. All the saloons were in dreadfully executive shades, too.' What the Vintage-minded chauvinists forgot was that Jaguar had 'gone executive', and had successfully effected the transformation. MkVII had proved itself a ministerial carriage, and the 3.4-litre had married XK performance to those 'Edwardian library' interiors praised by the weekly press. If the tragic death of Mike Hawthorn on the Guildford by-

Jaguar appeared at Le Mans, was a long-range, high-speed demonstration of technical progress staged at Monza by a team under Geoff Duke. The car was a nearly-standard 3.8-litre saloon with a 2.93:1 back axle and locked-out overdrive, and it ran for 10,000 miles at an average speed of 106.58mph – an improvement of more than 6mph on Leslie Johnson's marathon with the special-equipment XK120 in 1952.

'Black marks to Jaguar,' the *Veteran and Vintage Magazine* had howled in

A 3.8–litre Mk II police car of the type used in early British motorway days

pass had focussed attention on the compact's handling weaknesses, MkII had changed the picture once more. Many people still consider the 3.8-litre version to be the best saloon Jaguar have ever made, and this view indicates no deterioration in standards: it merely means that two-and-a-half years after their introduction the XJ6 series are still in short supply!

In the interests of economy the 240 of 1967–69 had neat grilles instead of fog lamps, and ambla rather than leather inside, but even at the age of thirteen it was competitive

RACING I

The first Jaguar XK 120s were a little short on brakes: ten years later the Jaguar was reckoned to be the best-braked car on the British market, and even MkX, the only post-war model to be greeted with modified rapture, invariably received full marks for its braking. In 1949 the XK series, at 160bhp, were not the world's most powerful series-production models: that honour went to Antoine Lago's GS-type Talbot, which ran to 190bhp. Yet by 1959 the Talbot was defunct, while the same Jaguar engine was giving 265bhp without any loss of reliability. Both XK and MkVII were advanced by the standards of their day, yet their basic engineering was still

competition Jaguar was made in 1963, the legacy survives. Disc brakes were first raced in 1952, were fitted to team cars as standard in 1953, and reached the regular range five years later. 1955 D-types had 285bhp engines which proved completely reliable: hence the touring unit's continuing ability to outlast more modern and expensive designs. In 1954 the original D-type had full unitary construction eighteen months before such methods penetrated to the production line. As for the E-type's revolutionary rear suspension, even this had been seen at Le Mans in 1960, on Briggs Cunningham's forgotten VKV 752, wearing the blue-and-white of America instead of the familiar Jaguar dark green.

Jaguar's racing programme was a curious one. They never won the Constructors' Championship. They never had enough cars to go round, though minor breakages could often be circumvented by the liberal use of 'stock' parts. Above all they worked, as William Heynes has himself admitted, with but one objective in view: to run the fastest scheduled service over the Sarthe Circuit that could be envisaged. Ferraris, Mercedes, Aston Martins were engineered to cover all the events of the season, from the twists and turns of the Nürburgring to the dusty open spaces of the Carrera Panamericana. Jaguar worked for Le Mans, and Le Mans alone: and this meant an engine capable of sustained high speed, manoeuvrability, and first-class brakes. Jaguar gearboxes and axles seldom broke (those on Ferraris quite often did so), and the cars were always driven to and from the circuit. These were the splendours; the principal miseries were imposed by the excellent surface at Le Mans, since Jaguar rear suspensions designed for billiard-table conditions were not up to

traditional. Within eleven years of the MkVII's introduction, the separate chassis was gone for good. Independent rear suspension still remains a controversial subject: but the last Jaguar with a beam axle was delivered in 1969.

Herein can be seen the influence of racing. The sport is expensive. Formulae exist to be 'bent' or evaded, and sometimes they are 'bent' so far that they lose all contact with reality. At one time only physical discomfort and a heavy fuel bill would deter enthusiasts from using sports-racers on the road: in the 1970s, by contrast, most racing saloons are not only noisy and uncomfortable, they are illegal. But there is no doubt that though the last

Not the easiest car to service: Leslie Johnson's XK 120 at the pits, Le Mans 1950

nastinesses such as the notorious Radicofani Pass on the Mille Miglia course. As the record shows, Jaguar surmounted these difficulties. Compare their Le Mans record from 1950 to 1957 with that of Ferrari. 1950 was a Talbot victory, in 1951 (Jaguar's first victorious year) the runners-up were again Talbot, and the Jaguar disaster of 1952 coincided with the resurgence of Mercedes-Benz. 1953 was a Jaguar benefit, with the sole surviving Ferrari in fourth place, and the tragedy of 1955 still left Jaguar in command of the situation once the Mercedes-Benz had withdrawn. 1956 saw the cars from Maranello beaten, not only by Jaguar, but also by Aston Martin, while 1957 was a splendid swansong, with the D-types swamping the entire opposition. Only in 1954 did a Ferrari win in a straight fight.

The story really opens with the 1950

Le Mans race. The SS 100, it is true, had distinguished itself in sprints, and some remarkable performances had been put up by drivers of the stamp of Tommy Wisdom and S H Newsome. An SS 100 was among the cars that would have contested the cancelled 1939 TT at Donington Park. Yet the marque's first success, way back in 1936, was not gained by a 100 but by a standard 2½-litre SS Jaguar tourer. In the Marne Grand Prix for sports cars F J McEvoy, an Australian amateur, won the 3-litre class at 69.98mph, from a brace of Amilcars, the oddly shaped four-cylinder Pégase models which were certainly good for 100mph.

The years passed, and nothing happened. As we have seen, the XK 120s of Johnson, Walker and Bira showed the flag in the 1949 Production Car Race at Silverstone, and it has been asserted that William Lyons was literally bullied into opening a competition department by his forceful Belgian distributor, Mme Bourgeois. Certainly the XK's racing debut in that country was marred by some appalling driving on the part of incompetent amateurs, but the facts suggest that the real trouble was that there were no cars to spare, so fierce was the export demand for the new model.

Across the Atlantic, of course, Jaguars were available, and in January 1950 Leslie Johnson finished fourth at Palm Beach after Bill Spear's sister car had lost its brakes. In May's Long Island races, however, the cars failed to match the acceleration of the Anglo-American Cadillac-Allards, and back in Europe the XKs which supported the Mille Miglia and the Targa Florio were also private entries. Nonetheless, it frightened the Italians to see the veteran Clemente Biondetti actually leading the Targa for a while on a Jaguar, even if three of the four XKs in the Mille Miglia retired. Johnson, however, took fifth place, less than an hour behind the winning Ferrari of Marzotto. This cannot have pleased the Italians either: by this time the Jaguar's competitive price was well known, but Marzotto had paid about £5,000 for his mount, and even a touring Ferrari was listed at £3,000.

The three standard XK 120s entered for Le Mans ran with the 'moral support' of the factory. Nobody, of course, backed them to win. Of 1949's stars Ferrari and Frazer Nash were back again, while the Lago-Talbots were firm favourites, Rosier's $4\frac{1}{2}$-litre being little more than a road-equipped Grand Prix machine. Allard had their Cadillac-engined J2, and a dark horse was the American Briggs Cunningham with a brace of Cadillacs, one of them an ugly open 'streamliner'.

The race went to Rosier, but not before the Johnson/Hadley Jaguar had kept going in uncanny silence for twenty hours, belying a best lap speed of 96.98mph. (The Talbot's fastest circuit had been just under 103mph).

Crowds on the road out of Brescia for the Mille Miglia, but there was something new and British in 1950: Clemente Biondetti's XK 120

Thereafter the XK's clutch packed up: its two team-mates were appreciably slower, but went the whole distance. A Jaguar victory in that year's TT was rather less significant, as the strongest opposition came from a 2-litre Frazer Nash. Nonetheless, it was important: it was the first major win by a works car, the first Jaguar victory in a long-distance race, and the first serious sports-car event for one of the world's greatest drivers, Stirling Moss. It was also won in pouring rain, which should have shown up any failings in the brakes, had they been serious. Peter Whitehead clinched matters with a second place for Jaguar.

1951 was, of course, to see the creation of a Competition Department proper under the management of F R W 'Lofty' England, Jaguar's Service Manager since 1946; an apposite choice since his long career as a racing mechanic had been spent in the service of Sir Henry Birkin, Whitney Straight, the ERA works team, Dick Seaman, and Bira. From now onwards the touring and competition strains of Jaguar were to divide. This was the heyday of the Appleyards and their white XK 120 roadster. Their Alpine Rally exploits merit a chapter in themselves, for the score was formidable. It started with a class win and best individual performance in 1950, a repeat in 1951 (plus a team award won in association with the Swiss drivers Habisreutinger and Soler), and an Alpine Gold Cup (something never previously awarded) for three consecutive clean sheets in 1952; the class victor that year was the

Dutchman Maurice Gatsonides, also on an XK 120. NUB 120 was retired in 1953 after winning the Morecambe Rally, but her successor, also an XK 120, netted the Appleyards another *coupé* that July. The original car, now with 50,000 miles on the clock, returned to the factory as a showpiece, and was subsequently lent to my museum at Beaulieu, along with one of the 1954 works D-types. As for club racing, the XK's successes were legion, and they lasted well into the 1960s.

1951 opened well with two production sports-car wins in Europe. The first of these fell to Johnny Claes in Belgium, his XK 120 beating eighty-three other cars, while the second was in the Bremgarten Preis at Berne. Neither the XK 120s nor Biondetti's odd Maserati-Jaguar special achieved anything in the Mille Miglia, but the new Competition Department's C-types

were unveiled in time for Le Mans.

Harry Weslake had been at work on the inlet porting and the exhaust system, and these improvements, allied to high-lift camshafts and a lightened flywheel, boosted output to 210bhp. For Le Mans a 3.31:1 axle ratio was used, though when the model was marketed a wide choice was available, from 2.9 to 4.27:1. The front suspension was unchanged; entirely new, however, were the tubular frame with its drilled side-members, the torsion-bar rear suspension, and the rack-and-pinion steering, not applied to touring models until 1955. Knock-off wire wheels replaced the XK 120's discs (which had slowed up pitwork in 1950), and the entire bonnet assembly hinged up for easy servicing. The catalogued weight of an XK 120 was 22 cwt; C-types turned the scales at only $18\frac{1}{2}$ cwt. In road-going trim the car would do 144mph, climb a 1-in-10 hill at 100 in top gear, and accelerate from a stand-still to 100mph in twenty seconds. An example tested by *The Motor* also successfully negotiated Brussels without wetting its plugs; the full-width bodywork could, at a pinch, accommodate weekend baggage for two; and 16 mpg was possible.

At Le Mans the factory fielded three cars (Johnson/Biondetti, Whitehead/Walker, and Moss/Fairman). These were up against three 4.1-litre Ferraris (Chinetti, Chiron and Spear); three of the new Chrysler-engined Cunninghams (Huntoon, Rand, and Fitch); and the usual Talbots and Allards, with the Nash-Healey and DB2 Aston Martin as likely outsiders. As it turned out, the Talbots were their strongest opponents, though the fastest Cunningham (Fitch's) challenged strongly and lay third for a while, before the big vee-eight engine started to burn its valves on the indifferent fuel, said to be seventy octane. At the fifth hour, it looked like a 1-2-3 Jaguar procession, an astonishing performance for a new model's first outing. Alas, Biondetti's car lost its oil pressure, and Moss's threw a rod at Arnage, leaving Whitehead and Walker

Above: Le Mans, 1951. Jaguar's first winning pair, Peter Whitehead and Peter Walker, in relaxed mood. Below: 'Laureaux a la Jaguar.' Peter Whitehead brings his C-type across the line after winning the 1951 Le Mans Race at 93.49mph

to scoop the pool. This they did at 93.49mph, finishing seventy-seven miles ahead of the Meyrat/Mairesse Talbot which took second place. To this could be added third in the Index of Performance (virtually the preserve of France's Panhard-based miniatures), and the fastest lap recorded by Moss before his retirement. Back home Jaguar's achievements collected them their second Malcolm Campbell Memorial Trophy in succession – the first had been won by Ian Appleyard for his Alpine exploits. They also won the RAC's Dewar Trophy.

After this the TT was fairly easy going with only the DB3 Aston Martin and two privately-entered Ferraris to beat,

Scotland that year were a C-type and four XK 120s. Though on occasion the Scottish Jaguars were to outstrip the Coventry entries, the two teams remained entirely independent of each other. Unquestionably, however, Murray and Wilkinson benefited greatly from Jaguar's know-how, and they were always given first refusal on the previous year's team machines.

In addition to Ian Stewart and the existing drivers (Moss, Whitehead and Walker) Jaguar signed up Duncan Hamilton. They could also look forward to stronger opposition. Of 1951's crop, Aston Martin, Healey, Ferrari, Talbot and Cunningham were still in the game. The newcomers included Amédée

even if the latest Aston proved nearly as fast as the C-types. Hall's Ferrari crashed, and the Baird/Hawthorn car could do no better than sixth, leaving Stirling Moss to win from his team-mate Peter Walker.

.The C-type figured in the 1952 Jaguar catalogue at £2,327, and the new season opened with the formation of a famous equipe, the Edinburgh-based Ecurie Ecosse. The original drivers were David Murray (the head of the organisation), Bill Dobson, Ian Stewart, and Sir James Scott Douglas, though Stewart also drove for the Jaguar works. The Ecosse cars were prepared by W E Wilkinson, and the five machines which wore the dark blue of

A winning car demands top drivers. Stirling Moss in characteristic pose on the way to victory in the 1951 TT

Gordini, who had finally severed his connection with Simca. Mercedes-Benz were back in racing for the first time since the war with the interesting 3-litre overhead-camshaft 300SL coupé, and there were also new sports models from FIAT and Alfa-Romeo. The former's 2-litre 8V never ventured outside national events, however, while the Alfa *dischi volanti* suffered from inadequate development, though they were very fast while they were going.

There were no works Jaguars in Florida for the opening round of the

Part of the victorious team at Le Mans, 1953. Tony Rolt avenged his 1952 retirement

tails and streamlined noses with diminutive air intakes, and though the radiators were later enlarged, these intakes were not. Within three hours of the start the entire Jaguar team had boiled itself out of business.

Nor were they destined to have their revenge over Mercedes in the Monaco sports-car race: the Germans did not enter. Ferrari did, however, turn out, and Jaguar might have beaten them, but for a monumental pile-up which eliminated not only Moss but also Manzon's Gordini and Parnell's Aston Martin. Neither Germans nor Italians supported the Rheims race, so Jaguar's

season, the Sebring Twelve Hours, and thus the Schott/Carroll XK 120's second place was creditable. Only Sir James Scott Douglas in an Ecosse XK 120 and Duncan Hamilton in his own C-type turned up for the British Empire Trophy Race in the Isle of Man. This was anything but a Jaguar circuit, though the Scots driver came in sixth. There were no Jaguars at Berne, either: the result was a Mercedes benefit, and the usual dedication to the cause of Le Mans prevented the Coventry equipe from sending more than a solitary C-type (Moss) to Italy for the Mille Miglia. This one, of course, marked the competition debut of the disc brake. It was well up among the leaders at Bologna, but damaged steering caused its retirement, and the race became a battle between Bracco's Ferrari and Kling's Mercedes-Benz. The Italian won. Unfortunately the impressive speed of the new German contenders frightened Jaguars into making a bad mistake at Le Mans. Four weeks before the race the C-types were given longer

88

victory was an empty one, especially after Manzon crashed his Gordini and left Moss on the disc-braked car to win from Mairesse's Talbot and Scott Douglas's XK 120. A run of bad luck was completed by Britain's first night race, the Goodwood Nine Hours. The opposition came from Aston Martin, Ferrari and Talbot, and misfortunes were fairly evenly shared between the two British teams. Parnell's Aston burnt itself out in the pits, the Whitehead/Stewart Jaguar ran out of road, and Rolt's C-type lost a wheel. The battle between the two surviving rivals, Moss and the Collins/Griffith Aston Martin, ended when the Jaguar's rear axle locating arm broke.

But the disc brakes had been proven, and were ready for 1953. Gone were the early days of trial at Silverstone, when calipers flexed, servos packed up, and the fluid boiled. It was, perhaps, a disappointment to 'Lofty' England and his team at Coventry to hear that Mercedes-Benz had decided to retire for the time being, but as usual Jaguar reserved everything for Le Mans. Only privately-owned cars were seen at Sebring, the Johnston/Wilder car finishing third on distance and seventh on formula. Both the works entries for the Mille Miglia (driven by Moss and Rolt) were 1952 cars with the addition of

A rare picture of a C-type in action at Tertre Rouge in the 1952 Le Mans race. The new noses played havoc with the cooling, and after three hours there were no Jaguars left

Stirling Moss leads a Ferrari at Le Mans, 1953

disc brakes, though Leslie Johnson used a five-speed overdrive box on his private entry. It was all to no avail: neither these nor the supporting Mk VIIs in the touring-car category got anywhere.

The 1953 C-types were, however, ready in good time for Le Mans. The twin SU carburetters had given way to a triple-Weber installation boosting power to 220bhp, and 2cwt had been pared off by the use of light-alloy radiators, small-diameter frame tubes, and lightweight bodies. Disc brakes were, of course, fitted to the works entries (Rolt/Hamilton, Moss/Walker, and Whitehead/Stewart). A fourth, Belgian-entered car (Laurent/de Tornaco) was a catalogued model with drums.

The opposition was formidable. Ferrari's fastest car was a $4\frac{1}{2}$-litre (Ascari/Villoresi), backed by three 4.1-litres (Farina/Hawthorn, Marzotto/Marzotto,

and Chinetti/Cole). Aston Martin had their new lightened 2.9-litre DB3S models, good for 180bhp, while the Cadillac-Allards had acquired aerodynamic coachwork. The 3-litre supercharged vee-six Lancias were considered to have a good chance, Fangio and Marimon led the team of fast *disco volante* Alfa-Romeos, and a team of revised and far lighter 5.4-litre Cunninghams (Cunningham/Spear, Walters/Fitch, and Moran/Benett) were well worth watching. After Pierre Levegh's narrow defeat in 1952, his $4\frac{1}{2}$-litre Talbot was likely to make the running, and Gordini's new $2\frac{1}{2}$-litre six, like the Alfas, was extremely fast as long as it stayed in one piece. Practice times on the Mulsanne Straight showed that the Cunninghams were the fastest, closely matched by Alfa-Romeo and Jaguar, with the Lancias nearly 15mph slower.

An early challenge by Sydney Allard was soon over, while fuel-feed trouble forced Moss's Jaguar back to fifteenth place, leaving Rolt and Hamilton to make the running against the real opposition – the Ferraris of Villoresi and Chinetti, two Alfa-Romeos, and the fastest Cunningham. By 8pm Hawthorn's Ferrari and Fangio's Alfa were out, as were two Talbots, but the remaining Alfa-Romeos lay in third and fourth places, even if the Ferrari challenge was reduced to one car, the extremely rapid 4½-litre now driven by Ascari. Twice the Ferrari snatched the lead, only to lose it in an extraordinary game in which the British car's superb brakes were used to force the Italians to crowd the pace on beyond their machine's endurance.

By early morning the Alfa-Romeos were out, and Jaguars lay first, fourth and fifth, the Moss/Walker crew having steadily made up all their lost time. Rolt was playing cat-and-mouse with Ascari until the Ferrari expired, leaving the Jaguars to make a processional finish. Rolt and Hamilton were still thirty miles ahead of Moss and Walker on the second car. But it was not to be 1-2-3, for the Fitch/Walters Cunningham

managed to interpose itself in third place : a gallant effort by America. Only two teams, Jaguar and Cunningham, finished intact. In this, the first Le Mans 24-Hour Race to be won at over 100mph, no fewer than seven cars had broken this 'barrier'.

There were more Jaguar successes to come. Duncan Hamilton had no luck at either Oporto or Pescara, but Moss and Whitehead won at Reims against Cunningham and Ferrari, and Ecurie Ecosse gained two useful second places at Spa (Scott Douglas/Gale) and at the Nürburgring (Stewart/Salvadori). Failing oil pressure eliminated the works cars in the Goodwood Nine Hours, which went to Aston Martin, and clutch trouble wrecked Jaguar's chances in the TT, or would have but for the skill of Stirling Moss, who kept his C-type going until two laps from the end, and then

The Isle of Man was no place for Jaguars : an Ecurie Ecosse car during the 1953 British Empire Trophy Race

pushed it across the line to take fourth place.

This put Jaguar in the lead for the Constructors' Championship, with only the Carrera Panamericana as the decider. Admittedly Jaguar were not going to Mexico and Ferrari were, but this 'automotive Grand National' was anybody's race and there was no guarantee that it would yield Ferrari the vital points. Alas for Jaguar, the Italian equipe won.

Already Jaguar Specials were making their appearance. In addition to Clemente Biondetti's effort in Italy, there were Oscar Moore's HWM-Jaguar, Philip Scragg's Alta-Jaguar, and Frank Le Gallais's rear-engined LGS sprint car in Jersey. Gordon Parker built himself a sprint sports car, the Jaguara, with Lotus-like lines and a twin-blown XK engine, while in America one enthusiast's idea of a perfect fast tourer (though not, of course, for competitions!) was a classic Lincoln Continental of the 1940s with XK power. What is more, Norman Buckley had introduced the name of Jaguar to a new element.

Originally Buckley's racing Ventnor speedboat had used a 4-litre six-cylinder Lycoming engine, but at the

end of 1949 he acquired a 3.4-litre XK unit, and converted it to magneto ignition. With this combination he annexed the one-hour record in the 800-kilogram class at 55.55mph, the prelude to a long marine career on Jaguar-powered boats. 1953 saw the Jaguar unit transferred to a new Canadian 'prop-riding' hull, and this Miss Windermere III proved capable of 100mph. Buckley's marine developments inspired other boat-racers (among them the German von Mayenburg) to adopt the twin-cam Jaguar engine, and down the years he continued to up-rate his power unit. In 1959 guise Miss Windermere used a 3.8-litre dry-sump D-type motor developing 300bhp and she managed a formidable

120.63mph over the kilometre.

Thus 1953 came to a close. Jaguar now had two Le Mans victories to their credit, and the latest C-types were passed on to Ecurie Ecosse. But before the year was out, people had had a sight of an interesting aerodynamic prototype. Photographs of this had been published before the Le Mans race, but precious little information was forthcoming. One thing was known, though. In October Norman Dewis, the factory's head tester, had taken it to Jabbeke, where he had been timed at 178mph, a good 30mph ahead of the C-type's best form.

Would this be Jaguar's 1954 contribution to Le Mans ?

RACING II

D-type underbonnet, 1954: three twin-choke Webers, dry-sump lubrication and 250bhp

Mercedes-Benz stayed out of racing in 1954, but to balance this Lancia were becoming more competition-minded. Jaguar-based specials were no longer a rarity, and among these were the RGS-Atalanta, based on the all-independently-sprung Atalantas made at Staines before the war: the HWM-Jaguars using Formula II chassis: and later some excellent sports-racers made by Cooper of Surbiton and Lister of Cambridge. Even the sole surviving E-type ERA of 1939 was to make a farewell appearance as a 'sports' car with road equipment and an XK engine in place of the $1\frac{1}{2}$-litre Riley-type unit. Jaguar, of course, could not be expected

to supply engines to potential rivals, though they were prepared to supply them in strictly limited quantity to special customers. These were eventually to include Sydney Allard, an erstwhile rival, but by 1956 the Cadillac-Allard's day was done and the Clapham firm were turning out a few cars to special order. The last one was made in 1959.

The new season got away to a good start with Mrs Anderson winning the

94

Australian 24-Hour Race on an XK 120 coupé after the Whitehead/Gaze C-type had retired. Ecurie Ecosse tried their luck in Buenos Aires, but managed nothing better than fourth, behind two Ferraris and an Aston Martin. Nor was the British Empire Trophy rewarding: it had been transferred to another tricky circuit, Cheshire's Oulton Park, and Duncan Hamilton's C-type was defeated by Peter Gammon's 1½-litre Lotus – an omen for the future. Not that all the omens were unfavourable to Jaguar, for in the *formule libre* race at Ibsley James Stewart (elder brother of a future World Champion) took second place behind a fading star, the legendary V-16 Formula I BRM. As for the International Trophy Meeting at Silverstone, this merely clinched something that Jaguars knew already: the C-type at the peak of its form was no match for the latest wear in Ferraris. Nor, for that matter, was David Brown's latest, a 12-cylinder car carrying the Lagonda crest.

A month before Le Mans the world had a sight of the 1954 competition Jaguar. This was not, of course, the 1953 streamliner, though the two types had quite a lot in common, among them the monocoque hull built around a centre-section of immense strength. The engine and front suspension were supported by an integral front section, and the tail assembly was bolted to the centre-section. The usual torsion bars at the front were matched by a live axle, trailing arms, and torsion bars at the rear. But while the 1953 hybrid had retained the C-type unit, the lessons of Goodwood had been learned, and the D-type's three-carburetter engine had dry-sump lubrication. In this guise it developed 250bhp. The four-speed synchromesh gearbox had extremely high ratios. Top was 2.79 to 1, and bottom 5.98. As usual a wide choice was to be available; on the hilly Agadir circuit Duncan Hamilton used a 4.09 axle, and with the highest ratios available (as at Le Mans in 1955) speeds of close on 200mph could be obtained. Steering and brakes were inherited from the

C-type, and numerous stock parts were incorporated. These included the cylinder block and head castings, the propeller shaft and the Salisbury rear axle.

The C-type had resembled the super-sports car that it was, but the new 'D', with its small oval air intake, streamlined headrest, and curved Perspex screen, looked every inch a racer. This did not stop the D-types from being driven to races whenever time permitted. Duncan Hamilton drove his from Casablanca to Agadir during the Moroccan season, and though Max Trimble preferred to use a trailer 'to avoid the risk of accident', his by-no-means-new D-type behaved well in traffic, returning 20mpg as against the C-type's best of 18mpg, thanks to superior aerodynamics. When a 1954 team car was displayed at the 1958 Geneva Show, Bob Berry, then Jaguar's Assistant Public Relations Officer, drove it out from Coventry: it was a cold passage in February, but otherwise uneventful. The new racer was far more compact than its forebears. Frontal area was drastically reduced, six inches were lopped off the wheelbase, and seven inches off the overall length. In preliminary tests at Le Mans Rolt did a standing lap at 107mph and a flying lap at 115.6mph, faster than Ascari's best on a Ferrari in 1953. On the Mulsanne Straight the D-type's 169mph compared favourably with the previous year's best, 154.81mph by John Fitch on a Cunningham. For an equipe which had won on brakes, this was an encouraging outlook, and to the practical Jaguar mind such a dummy run was infinitely more profitable than a trip to the Mille Miglia with still-untried cars. There were no D-types in the Italian marathon.

What had the opposition to offer? Briggs Cunningham's heavyweights were back again, supported by a Cunningham-prepared Ferrari. Aston Martin, while relying principally on the DB3S, threw in a blown coupé and the V-12 Lagonda for good measure. Gordini had three twin-cam sixes (one

Duncan Hamilton (far left) and Tony Rolt: 1st at Le Mans in 1953, and 2nd in 1954

of them a 2.9-litre), Maserati also favoured six cylinders, and the Ferrari stud embraced everything from a modest 3-litre to five litres and 340bhp of 'vee-twelve. Absentees were Alfa-Romeo, who had abandoned the unequal struggle with their *dischi volanti*, and Lancia, preoccupied with Formula I. The three works Jaguars were entrusted to Moss/Walker, Hamilton/Rolt and Whitehead/Wharton.

In the event, the Jaguars had the better braking ability and straight-line speed, and Ferrari had the edge on acceleration, but this time acceleration told, despite the fact that Maranello's fastest car was flat out at 160mph. By midnight the 4½-litre Ferrari of Maglioli/Marzotto had spent itself after lying second, though all the Jaguars were dogged by misfiring. Moss's brakes failed, putting him out of the race, and the Whitehead/Wharton team (already reduced to one gear ratio – top!) gave up with cylinder head trouble. The Rosier/Manzon Gordini broke its gearbox, the supercharged Aston expired at noon on the second day, and in the last few hours it was one Ferrari (Gonzalez/Trintignant) versus one Jaguar, with a three-mile gap at the end. Both the leaders averaged 105mph, so Britain only just lost. The Spear/Johnston Cunningham was third, and a C-type driven by the Belgians Laurent and Swaters came in fourth.

At Hyeres the all-independently-sprung Cooper-Jaguar of Whitehead retired, but in the absence of Aston Martin and the works Ferraris the D-types had an easy time at Reims, though Moss went out after making the fastest lap. The Laurent/Swaters C-type, however, took third place behind the works cars of Whitehead and Rolt.

William Lyons (right) and W M Heynes keep an eye on the scheduled service in the Jaguar pit at Le Mans, 1954

Everyone contested the TT at Dundrod, not that the heavy brigade had any real chance of victory in a race run under 'Index of Performance' rules. The laurels went, predictably, to a little air-cooled DB-Panhard, ahead of two Ferraris. Jaguar, who had tried to beat the formula with a 2½-litre engine in one of their cars, were rewarded with wholesale retirement. A notable success was Ninian Sanderson's second place for Ecurie Ecosse (still, of course, using C-types) in the Dutch sportscar race at Zandvoort.

Mercedes-Benz returned to the fray in 1955 with a straight-eight, the 300SLR, based on their W196 Grand Prix machine, but they were not ready for Sebring in March, though Ferrari, Maserati and Cunningham were. Briggs Cunningham, however, did better with his newly acquired D-type than with his own Meyer-Drake engined 3-litre machine, so it was first blood to Jaguar. The successful partnership was Hawthorn/Walters.

Aston Martin came out on top at Silverstone in June, Jaguar having to rest content with class honours, but the Ulster Trophy Race was a Jaguar double, Titterington's Ecurie Ecosse D-type winning on speed, and W T Smith's C-type on handicap.

Le Mans 1955 has, of course, gone down in history because of the appalling accident in which Levegh's Mercedes-Benz collided with Macklin's Austin-Healey, killing eight spectators and injuring over a hundred more. It was also a meeting of the principal contestants: the Mercedes with their air-brakes, led by the unbeatable combination of Fangio and Moss, two 3-litre Maseratis, and a brace of Ferraris (Maglioli/Farina and Trintignant/Schell). Cunningham hedged his bets with a D-type Jaguar and his own 3-litre car, Aston Martin ran the Lagonda as well as their usual DB3S models, and the Whitehead brothers fielded a Cooper-Jaguar. The three works D-types (Rolt/Hamilton, Hawthorn/Bueb, and Beauman/Dewis) were also new.

Le Mans, 1954. The heavy metal sorts itself out, but already D-type numbers 15 (Whitehead/Wharton) and 12 (Moss/Walker) are showing their form

A less costly form of structure was utilised, incorporating a separate steel-tube sub-frame, and there was a second oil pump to lubricate the gearbox. Wider screens and more powerful 285bhp engines completed the specification, and the axle ratio was raised to 2.53 : 1. By this time, of course, the model was on sale to the public with 1955's structural revisions, but retaining the short nose, headrest, and less potent engine of the previous year. List price was £3,878, and forty-eight were delivered before production ceased in 1957.

After the tragedy the surviving Mercedes-Benz were withdrawn early on the second day, when Moss and Fangio led, and it is still a matter of controversy whether in happier circumstances Jaguar would have won. On balance, this seems likely, for the Hawthorn/Bueb partnership not only took the chequered flag at 107mph, but also set a new course record with a lap at 122.387mph. A final note of tragedy was struck when John Lyons, William Lyons' only son, met his death in a road accident *en route* for Le Mans. He had only recently gone to work at Jaguars after serving an apprenticeship with Leyland Motors. In the wake of disaster race after race was cancelled, while circuit-owners feverishly sought to overhaul their safety regulations. Ultimately the casualties were to include the Mille Miglia, though it took another terrible crash to kill the Italian classic.

Of the surviving events in the calendar, Aintree was too short and tricky a course even for a driver of Mike Hawthorn's calibre, and he had to be content with fourth place on the works

It can rain at Reims, too. The victorious Whitehead/Wharton car roars through the murk, 1954

Tony Rolt hard at work with a D-type, Le Mans 1954

D-type, behind all three works Astons. With only a privately-owned C-type to oppose them, Mercedes-Benz scored an easy victory in Sweden, but though Aston Martin won the Goodwood Nine Hours again, Titterington and Sanderson came second for Jaguar and Ecurie Ecosse, the formidable 750S Ferraris of Hawthorn and de Portago proving unreliable in the extreme. Ferrari won the International Trophy at Oulton, with Bob Berry's D-type a good fourth.

finish at Watkins Glen, and had his revenge on Hill, at an average of 87.9mph, in the President's Cup at Hagerstown.

1956 saw some good performances in New Zealand. The star of these was Leslie Marr's Connaught-Jaguar, a re-engined 1955 Grand Prix car, though Tony Gaze's HWM-Jaguar won the Ardmore sports-car race from two XK 120s. At Sebring four D-types ran under Briggs Cunningham's sponsorship, and though output was now up to 300bhp, the new petrol-consumption rules imposed at Le Mans were re-

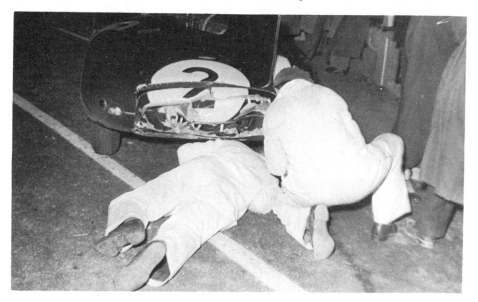

Hamilton's car in the pits at night, showing damage after Behra's Gordini had rammed co-driver Rolt in the stern

Mercedes collected the first three places in the TT, but the moral victor was Hawthorn, who gave the Germans a terrific run for their money. Before the D-type's engine blew up on the penultimate lap, the British driver had passed Fangio to take second place, and he had never been further back than third. In America Sherwood Johnston had a magnificent season with Briggs Cunningham's car. If Phil Hill's Ferrari beat him at Elkhart Lane, he led from start to

12 hours of Reims, 1954. Duncan Hamilton leading the Whitehead/ Wharton D-type

flected in the use of fuel injection, first tested on a C-type in 1954. Unfortunately the brake fluid and the hot Floridian climate just did not mix, and disaster struck. The unhappy Bueb was stuck in the pits when his brakes refused to free, and then ran out of road when they refused to go on. Hawthorn kept going for eight of the twelve hours, holding fourth place without any anchors at all, and the only comfort was

a third (behind two Ferraris) for Bob Sweikert, victor of the 1955 Indianapolis 500-Mile Race.

Graham Whitehead gained a fifth at Dakar, but the Oulton Park handicappers destroyed Jaguar's chances, though they could not prevent Flockhart from scoring a record sports-car lap at 84.95mph. A win for Guyot in one of the Mille Miglia's countless production-car classes was a pleasant surprise, and in the Coupe de Paris at Montlhéry Hamilton's D-type not only beat the latest in Grand Prix Gordinis, but also a full-house racing Maserati. There were more minor wins, and this year the big battalions met first at Reims, Le Mans having been postponed to allow the circuit to be reconstructed. Here transmission disorders eliminated both the Monza Ferrari and the 350S Maserati, leaving the works D-type of Hamilton/ Bueb to take the honours. Hawthorn and Frère finished second for Jaguar, with

Another wet Le Mans : the tragic 1955 race. In the pits, the winning D-type of Hawthorn/Bueb

Night racing in Britain: a D-type at speed in the 1955 Goodwood Nine Hours

Ecurie Ecosse entries in third and fourth places.

Full-width screens were demanded for Le Mans, while the fuel-consumption rules meant at least 11.5mpg for Jaguar, who countered with some more weight reduction and (in the case of the works cars) fuel injection. Ecurie Ecosse, who entered only one machine (MWS 301, for Flockhart/Sanderson) preferred conventional carburetters. Aston Martin had a new $2\frac{1}{2}$-litre DBR 1, entrusted to team-leader Parnell. Ferrari's Testa Rossas of like capacity were also new, and Gordini's familiar sixes were supported by a straight-eight based on the racing single-seater. Talbot were also back in the game, though they had adopted the $2\frac{1}{2}$-litre Maserati engine in place of the old Becchia-designed $4\frac{1}{2}$-litre.

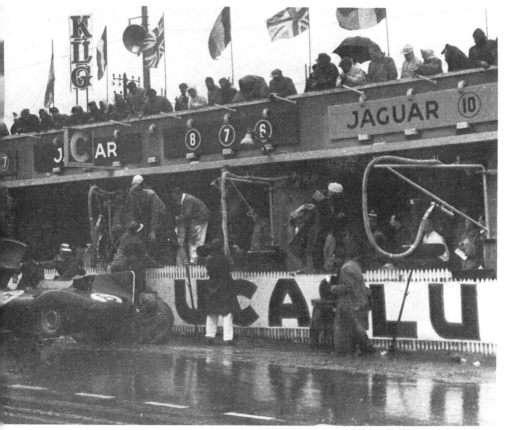

It was a bad day for the works
Jaguars. A hair-crack in one of the fuel-
feed pipes of Hawthorn's car lost him
twenty precious laps, and his ultimate
sixth place was won only by driving of
true championship standard. A crash on
the second lap eliminated Fairman and
Frère before they could make the running, which left only the car from
Edinburgh to challenge the field. And
this year the battle was to be an all-
British one, against the Moss/Collins
DB3S Aston, and it was a real needle
match. The winning Jaguar's average
was 104.46mph to the Aston Martin's
104.04mph, with the Gendebien/Trin-

tignant Ferrari third. A Belgian-entered D-type took fourth place.

It was sad that Sebring and Le Mans,
perhaps Hawthorn's greatest drives for
Jaguar, were relatively so unsuccessful,
but he was destined to die at the wheel
of his 3.4-litre on the Guildford by-pass
after he had won the 1958 World
Championship and announced his retirement from the circuits.

In October 1956 Jaguar decided to
give up racing. 'Lofty' England returned to his main role as Service
Director, and the team cars were passed on to Ecurie Ecosse. The only sign
of anything really sporting from

Allesley was the XK-SS, a road-going development of the D-type of which only sixteen were made. A few amenities were added : these included a hood, a full-width screen, side windows, a luggage-grid and vestigial bumpers, while the dorsal fin was deleted. The car shared the production D-type's 250-bhp dry-sump engine with carburetters, and it offered 144mph, not to mention acceleration likened by one writer to 'a rocket-propelled sledge', or in cold sprint 0-100mph in 14.4 seconds, and 0-120mph in less than twenty seconds. Thanks to the race-bred brakes, it was possible to hold 120mph

Prelude to a duel. At the start of the 1955 TT Hawthorn's D-type and Moss's Mercedes-Benz are already nosing out ahead

on a straight stretch and then ease the XK-SS into a succession of corners at 60-70mph. American customers paid $5,750 for these way-out pleasures : Britons did without.

But if the factory was out of the game, independents fought on. Hawthorn and Bueb shared the wheel of Cunningham's Sebring entry, the first car with the 3,781cc engine, and took third place behind a pair of Maseratis. This was

Above: The year the brakes boiled: Hawthorn at speed in the D-type at Sebring, 1956. Below: The Flockhart/Sanderson Ecurie Ecosse D-type on the way to victory, Le Mans 1956

Above: The Lister–Jaguar is indelibly associated with the late Archie Scott-Brown, but here is Philip Scragg manipulating his 3.8–litre hill–climb version at Prescott, 1961. Below: Limited edition for export. The 1957 XK-SS was nearly a D-type despite the elaborate silencing system

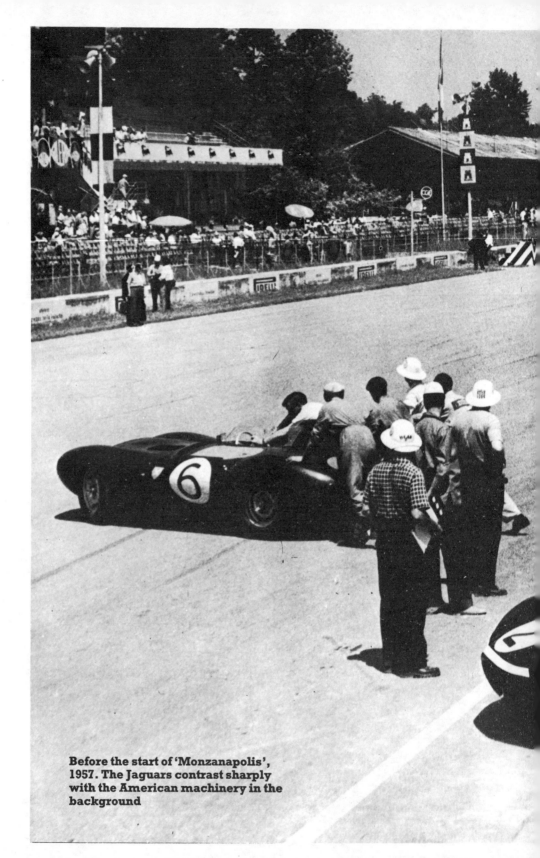

**Before the start of 'Monzanapolis',
1957. The Jaguars contrast sharply
with the American machinery in the
background**

**Above left: Typical of the Jaguar-powered specials is this monoposto HWM-Jaguar, seen during AF Rivers Fletcher's ownership. The car started life as one of the Hersham firm's Formula II single seaters
Left: Wearing the blue-and-white: the experimental 3-litre car, VKV 752, which Briggs Cunningham ran at Le Mans 1960. Above: D-type postscript how Michelotti dressed it up for the 1963 Geneva Salon**

neither the first nor the last Jaguar racing unit with non-standard cylinder dimensions. As well as the 2½-litre used in the 1954 TT there had also been a 3-litre tried at Rouen in 1956. All these variants (with one exception, a 'bored and stroked' 2.4 of 3,000cc campaigned by Ecurie Ecosse in 1960) were factory jobs. Another 1957 novelty was Brian Lister's latest creation, the 3.4-litre Lister-Jaguar with twin-tube frame, all-round disc brakes, and the combination

of coil-and-wishbone front suspension with a de Dion back axle. This subsequently ran in 3.8-litre form, and won the one-armed Archie Scott-Brown sixteen firsts and two seconds in one-and-a-half seasons, before his tragic death in May 1958.

1957 saw the last Mille Miglia, which Ecurie Ecosse supported unsuccessfully. Third and fourth places represented Jaguar's best at Spa, and at the Nürburgring the results ran to form, with an Aston Martin victory, and the best Jaguar (Flockhart/Fairman) well back in seventh. Le Mans, likewise, had everyone guessing, for the latest regulations stipulated 92-octane fuel, adequate weather protection (some of the attempts at conformity were as comical as they were useless!), and screens with a minimum height of fifteen centimetres. With the works no longer competing, the Jaguar challenge was of course dependent on existing D-types, but improvements included

111

new brakes with quick-replaceable pads, and two of the Ecurie Ecosse cars wore new 3.8-litre fuel-injection engines. The windscreens took no less than 10mph off the top speed.

Further, the opposition had gone to town. Aston Martin's DBRs (destined to win the 1959 Constructors' Championship) were more powerful than ever, a brace of 2.9-litre machines being joined by a 3.7-litre. Maserati's challengers were 4-litre four-ohc vee-eights said to be good for 400bhp: one of these was cloaked in a strange-looking Zagato coupé body styled by Frank Costin. Their five-speed gearboxes lived in the back axles, and the team leader was Stirling Moss, partnered by Harry Schell. Mike Hawthorn's 4-litre Ferrari also ran to four upstairs camshafts, though this was of course a V-12 and output was quoted at a more modest 380bhp, and as a second-string Maranello ran a brace of 3.8-litre machines. Of the five Jaguars, Ecurie Ecosse contributed three, the other two being standard D-types entered by Los Amigos of France (Lucas/'Mary') and Equipe Nationale Belge (Frère/Rousselle).

The result was a walk-over for Jaguars who finished first, second, third, fourth and sixth. Of the Aston Martins, only Tony Brooks was ever in the picture, and he crashed while lying second. As for the Italian demonstration of brute force, it fell to pieces – almost literally. The gearbox of Moss's Maserati lasted less than an hour, Simon crashed the open 4-litre, and Hawthorn's Ferrari expired in a cloud of smoke. Before midnight two more cars were out of action; the 3-litre Maserati of Scarlatti/Bonnier broke its transmission, and one of the 3.8-litre Ferraris broke a piston. After that it was Jaguar all the way – Flockhart and Bueb first at 113.85mph, followed home by Sanderson/Lawrence (111.15mph), Lucas/'Mary' (110.17mph), and Frère/Rousselle (107.95mph). There was some comfort in Lewis-Evans' and Severi's fifth for Ferrari, and the Bianchi/Harris 2-litre was seventh, with the last Jaguar

sandwiched in between. It was just like the good old days when 'WO's' Bentleys ruled the Sarthe Circuit.

After this anything would have been an anti-climax, and now that Rheims was given over to *granturismi* (understandably an XK 140 could make no impression in such company) the next item on the agenda for Jaguar was that extraordinary event which the calendar termed 'The Cup of Two Worlds', but which everyone else called 'Monzanapolis'. This was a 500-mile Indianapolis-style grind over the fast banked circuit at Monza. The regular supporters of Formula I racing firmly boycotted it, so that left a selection of Indianapolis machinery from the United States, and three Jaguar D-types from Ecurie Ecosse.

The outcome was predictable. America's best with their 4.2-litre fuel-injected Meyer-Drake four-cylinder engines and two-speed gearboxes were tailor-made for this kind of sport, whereas the British cars came straight from Le Mans. The fastest Jaguar's qualifying lap was done at 152mph: Jimmy Bryan, the American winner, *averaged* 160.1mph. But the Jaguar contingent cruised quietly round to take fourth, fifth and sixth places, prompting a rich American sponsor to mutter darkly: 'Hell, my car cost forty thousand bucks. These things I can buy around seven grand, I guess, and they are darn near as fast as mine.' The event was staged once more in 1958, and this time Brian Lister and David Murray collaborated to build a 3.8-litre single-seater for Jack Fairman to drive. It was no faster than the standard article, and though the team from Scotland gave their usual impressive demonstration, their best placing was Ivor Bueb's ninth.

Ecurie Ecosse soldiered on into 1958, but the odds were lengthening, especially in view of the new 3-litre capacity limit at Le Mans. There was another seventh place at the Nürburgring, but no reward at all in the TT, where the Jaguars proper gave way to Jaguar-engined machinery by Lister and Tojeiro. If Bueb annexed the first Scott-Brown Memorial Trophy Race at Snetterton on a Lister-Jaguar, and a C-type set a new sports-car record in the Brighton Speed Trials, the D-type could do no better than third in the Albert Park event in far-away Melbourne.

As for Le Mans, it was a pale shadow of 1957. Both Ecurie Ecosse and Duncan Hamilton preferred carburetters for their 3-litre engines, but though 95-100 octane fuel was now permitted, the reduced capacity knocked a further 20mph off the D-types' top speed. Piston failure eliminated both the Scottish entries, while Hamilton overturned when leading at the eight-hour mark.

Things were no better in 1959, though Lister made a new car with 3-litre engine and low-drag bodywork, and one of these, plus a brace of the 1958 models, ran at Sebring. All retired. At Silverstone's International Trophy Meeting, Bueb took third place on a works Lister, and none of the Jaguar contingent (two D-types, a Lister and a Tojeiro) lasted out the full twenty-four hours at Le Mans. The best showing was made by the Gregory/Ireland D-type, which held second place for a while.

A 3-litre limit also obtained in the *granturismo* category, and already the smaller cars were coming to the fore. A Lotus won Australia's Commonwealth TT, beating a Maserati and a D-type. Sebring's 1960 race attracted no Jaguars or Jaguar-engined cars, and in a GT race at Goodwood (where big cars were allowed) a 1,216cc Lotus Elite had the legs of an XK 150S, though Don Parker's similar car subsequently beat Sir Gawaine Baillie's Elite at Oulton Park. The Ecurie Ecosse D-types were further slowed by the latest rules which stipulated 'luggage boots' and touring-type windscreens. By Le Mans they were down to one D-type, now with their own brand of 'square' 3-litre engine: Brian Lister had given up making cars altogether. Briggs Cunningham was trying a new mount at Le

Mans in the shape of a Chevrolet Corvette.

He had, however, also entered something exciting – a 3-litre Jaguar. And a new one at that, for VKV 752 was in effect an E-type prototype. Here was a reversion to the full unitary construction of 1954 D-types, and in other respects the racing practice of the past was followed. The fuel-injected 3-litre engine disposed of 295bhp, but entirely new were a synchronised bottom gear (not offered on touring Jaguars until the 1965 season) and independent coil-and-wishbone rear suspension. The factory had turned the tiresome Appendix-C regulations to good purpose, by extending the statutory 'tonneau cover' so that it terminated behind the seats, and made the Cunningham car into a coupé.

Despite Hansgen's fastest practice lap, the old D-type went faster in the race. The American retired after the fuel-injection pipes had been damaged in a minor shunt, while Flockhart's and Halford's effort for Scotland came to an end when the crankshaft broke. VKV 752, however, was destined to race once more, at Elkhart Lake, where Hansgen drove it into third place behind a Ferrari and a Maserati. Though the Cunningham Jaguar equipe turned out for the US Grand Prix meeting, they fielded only 3.8-litre Mk II saloons, and were rewarded with a first and a second.

Thereafter the D-types faded out. But one of them, MWS 301, the victor of Le Mans, 1956, was destined to enjoy the limelight once more, though it was not the sort of limelight that anyone in Coventry or Edinburgh had envisaged.

On a hot August day fourteen years later, the Edward Gordon Thomson Collection came under the hammer at Perthshire's Gleneagles Hotel, and among the assortment of rare classics was the blue Jaguar. After a 'lap of honour' by Ninian Sanderson, the car changed hands for a resounding ten thousand pounds, and will stay in Scotland as a reminder of the great days at Le Mans.

CLASS
OF THE
SIXTIES

When a firm closes its competition department, it either means they cannot afford racing, or can afford not to race. With Jaguar, it was a combination of both in approximately equal measure. Their withdrawal in 1956 was logical: the D-type was nearing the end of its career, and in any case was being overtaken by a flood of regulations. It is equally true to say that the marque had well and truly arrived. The 'promenade car' image was safely buried before the C-type turned a wheel, and four wins at Le Mans had set the seal on Heynes' engine for good.

Alongside those who criticised Jaguar for abandoning the circuits, there was another small but vocal group who accused them of lapsing into a stereotyped mould. In 1960 there had been no big hit for three years, and even the last one, the 3.4-litre, had marked only a logical step from the 2.4-litre announced sixteen months earlier. Others craved for a return to traditional

E-types in the making, 1967. By this time capacity had gone up to 4.2 litres and a 2 +2 had joined the original roadster and coupé models

lines, but all the critics ignored one basic fact. Jaguar was a successful commercial enterprise which, in the manner of any specialist firm, catered for a minority. Catering for a minority within a minority would be an entirely different affair.

By 1960 the company was sitting pretty. They had sold nearly 21,000 cars in 1959. They had underwritten the problem of future expansion by buying the old-established Daimler concern for £3,400,000. This was truly a coup, for one of the penalties of a planned economy is that expanding businesses cannot always expand where they like. They are likely to be diverted into a 'development area' where only the wrong kind of labour is plentiful. Jaguar had bought production facilities 'just down the road', and if Daimlers' sales and finances alike were creaky, they brought with them two admirable vee-eight engines from the drawing-board of Edward Turner, and a useful line in diesel-powered 'buses. Nor did any of their existing cars clash with the Jaguar range. The two-seater SP 250 conveniently bridged a gap in the market between the XK 150 and machines of the calibre of Triumph's TR3 and the big Austin-Healey, while the Majestics were more akin to the 3-litre Rover and the dying Armstrong Siddeley than to any saloon Jaguar. Further, while almost the whole British motor industry lay in the grip of a recession and the fields around the big factories were cluttered with unsold cars, there was work for all at The Jaguar, and notices were displayed in the shops adjuring the workers not to be 'like the others'. The men and women at Browns Lane were not: the

spring of 1961 came round without a single day's short-time, and 1960's figures had been barely a thousand down on 1959's.

The biggest news of the New Year was, of course, technical rather than financial, for Jaguar's E-type produced the usual crop of well-merited super-latives, not all of them from the motoring press. *The Sunday Times* felt that it would 'go a long way towards repairing and restoring our slightly tarnished prestige throughout the world.' *The Motor* spoke of the 'admiration and envy' of Continental engineers, who would throw up their hands and ask (by no means for the first time) 'how Lyons does it'. *Motor Sport* called the E-type 'a stupendous achievement of British automobile engineering and crafts-manship'. As a boost to Britain's de-clining share of the Swiss market, Geneva was chosen as the scene of the new car's debut, whereupon film director Jacques Charrier (better known as the husband of Brigitte Bardot) flew from Rome to ensure a place at the head of the expected queue. Another customer who tried to book a demonstration at Jaguar's Piccadilly showrooms was firmly told that all the demonstrators were in Switzerland: he booked a flight to Geneva instead.

What manner of car was this? In fact the E-type, though a miracle, was not quite the revolution that its admirers suggested. Students of the marque's progress recognised it for what it was: a brilliant blend of many ideas the factory had been exploring for a decade.

The unitary hull (a Jaguar product, unlike that of the saloons) derived directly from the 1954 D-type. It was a welded and stressed shell of 20-gauge steel sheet, braced by box-section members which made up the door sills, scuttle assembly, propeller-shaft tunnel and cross-members. The detachable tubular front section carrying engine, steering-gear and front suspension was also of D-type origin, as were the suspension units themselves. At the

Filling a gap. The 1964 S-type looked a halfway house between the Mk II and the new independent rear-suspension models

rear, however, the inspiration was the 1960 Le Mans 3-litre, for an independently-sprung layout had been adopted, with twin coils, assisted by Girling telescopic dampers, and located by parallel transverse links of unequal length and longitudinal radius arms. For convenience of servicing and assembly this unit (including the inboard disc brakes) was mounted in a detachable bridge-piece. Rack-and-pinion steering and Dunlop disc brakes were a matter of course on a sporting Jaguar, and safety was assured in the case of the latter by the adoption of duplicated master cylinders.

The 3.8-litre wet-sump engine developed 265bhp, and came from the XK 150S, though two improvements were a new type of electric petrol pump immersed in the fuel tank, and an electrically-driven fan. The hypoid rear axle incorporated a limited-slip differential, and there were no transmission options: all E-types came with four-speed manual boxes. Bottom gear still lacked synchromesh. Bodywork

Enter twin headlamps, but the 1961 Mk X's almost-American proportions are still beautifully balanced

was fully aerodynamic, down to recessed headlamps, and buyers had the choice of a fixed-head coupé or a roadster, both designed for two people and their luggage. Triple wipers kept the curved screen clear in bad weather. Thanks to a curved, swing-up front section, underbonnet accessibility, hitherto a weak point on Jaguars, was now excellent. Wire wheels were standard: the only extras were radio, Dunlop R5 racing tyres, chromium-plated wheels, and a detachable hardtop on the open cars. The price? £2,097 for a coupé, inclusive of British purchase tax. £99 less would buy a roadster, and this at a time when the DB4 Aston Martin retailed for £3,775, and even the modest AC Aceca-Bristol cost £2,561. The Continental masterpieces, of course, were in an altogether higher bracket: £5,314 for a Mercedes-Benz 300SL, £6,024 for a Maserati 3500, and £6,326 for the cheapest Ferrari. These figures were inflated by duty, so a fairer comparison can be drawn from the figures ruling in Swit-

S-type in a party frock. Bertone's 1966 Jaguar sports saloon was probably the best attempt by an outside stylist, but it was too expensive for the market

zerland a couple of years later. Then an E-type sold for the equivalent of £2,175, by contrast with a Ferrari at £3,988. Chevrolet's fierce and much-improved Corvette, with all the resources of General Motors behind it, cost more than a Jaguar at £2,546.

Here indeed was something for world markets to digest. Five hundred orders were booked at Geneva alone, and the New York Importers' exhibition in April added another £11 million's worth to Jaguar's books. No wonder, for here was the fastest production touring Jaguar of all time, including the fabulous XK-SS. Top speed was 150mph, with 110mph or more available on third, and nearly 80mph on second. In terms of acceleration, although at low speeds a 1949 XK 120 could just

about keep pace, thereafter the gap widened. The new car would have been 1½ seconds ahead at 50mph, 3 seconds ahead at 60mph, and by the time the earlier model was doing 100mph the E-type would have settled down at 120mph. A 10-100mph acceleration time of 25 seconds on top gear alone was an astonishing demonstration of flexibility. Serious criticisms were confined to a 'slow' gearbox: once again Jaguar had come up with a winner capable of many years of steady development, and of supremacy. It is sobering to reflect that as late as 1968, 95 per cent of the E-type's output was earmarked for export, and 85 per cent of the cars went to North America.

The E-type was a 'grand tourer' if not quite a 'GT'. Its racing career, however, was not as significant as many people might have hoped. As early as April 1961, Graham Hill won the Oulton Park Trophy for Grand Touring Cars at 83.22mph, beating Ferraris and a DB4 GT Aston Martin, and in the early part of 1963 the limited-

production Lightweights made to special order by the factory gained a momentary ascendancy over the Ferraris in national events. But they were not destined to revive the tradition set by the XKs in their early years. Nonetheless, the Cunningham/Salvadori E-type took fifth place at Le Mans in 1962, and a race average of 108.87mph was an impressive milestone – in 1956 such a speed would have assured an outright win. Elsewhere, however, the extra brake horses of Ferrari's GTO were crucial, and in the TT Jaguar's best performance was a fourth. Le Mans, 1963, marked Briggs Cunningham's swansong after more than a decade, but he had to be content with ninth. Peter Lindner's staunch challenge at the Nürburgring ended in retirement.

Jaguars were to be seen, of course, in some very unlikely branches of the sport. In 1961 Tommy Lloyd won the British Stock-Car Championship on a nearly-standard XK 140 with 3.8-litre three-carburetter engine, and in 1967 a

Jaguar-powered dragster, the work of Virginian driver Roy Chambers, did a standing quarter-mile at 143.75mph. The same year saw the Bladon/Vyse 2½-litre Daimler saloon win the big-automatic class of the British Mobilgas Economy Run. It turned in 26.64mpg and beat examples of Ford, Vauxhall, Humber, Wolseley and Rover.

For 1962 MkIX gave way to MkX, and monocoque techniques at last invaded the prestige end of the Jaguar range. The new big saloon had independent coil-spring suspension at front as well as rear, and the structure, made up of two fabricated box-sections running the length of the 'body' and another box-section cross-member serving as a scuttle, was immensely rigid. Like the E-type MkX wore its rear disc brakes inboard, and it had the same 3.8-litre engine and Powr-Lok differential. Jaguar's three regular transmission options were continued, though all early MkXs were delivered with Borg-Warner automatic. New on a Jaguar was the four-headlamp installation, but once again the Lyons touch resulted in classical, unadorned proportions on a really large car, 196 inches long, 76 inches wide, and turning the scales at 35cwt. It was also a good 7mph faster than MkIX (at 120mph), and would attain 100mph in less time than it took an early MkVII to reach 90mph. I owned one of the first MkXs, and found it very thirsty indeed: but it was also incredibly quiet, and surefooted in a way that none of its predecessors had been. It could be thrown about as easily as the 3.8-litre MkII which it replaced. Such departures were becoming expensive, of course, and MkX cost Jaguars £4 million in tooling costs. This makes it all the more remarkable that 1961/2 profits rose by £216,000.

Jaguar were going all out for comprehensive coverage of the luxury market. In 1963 they had an impressive line-up. The MkII was available in four versions: 2.4-litre, 3.4-litre and 3.8-litre Jaguars, and the small vee-eight Daimler. MkX fulfilled the role of sporting carriage, and comparable performance plus a more stately aura was attainable with the 4.6-litre Daimler Majestic Major. A long-chassis edition of this latter contested the mayoral market against the British Motor Corporation's hoary 4-litre Vanden Plas Princess, now in its sixteenth year. For sports-car fans there was the Daimler SP 250 for only £1,355, and the incomparable E-type. There was still, however, a gap between the compact and executive groups, so the S-type was introduced for 1964.

This was in effect a MkII with restyled front end, twin rear tanks, enlarged boot, and independent rear suspension, available with 3.4-litre or 3.8-litre engine. Prices started at £1,669, but unfortunately this one took a long time to reach series production. More enthusiasm was generated by the 1965 newcomers, up-rated editions of the E-type and the MkX.

Already there were rumours of a vee-twelve, but once again the faithful twin-cam six was given a fresh lease of life, the latest 4,235cc version making use of a redesigned block with re-spaced bore centres. At the same time it was given alternator ignition, a pre-engaged starter motor, and revised ancillary drives, and a new type of oil-control ring cut down the unit's sometimes alarming thirst for lubricant. It was noted that while capacity went up, output did not: instead, owners reaped the benefit of superior bottom-end torque and acceleration in the middle-speed range.

Even better was a new all-synchro-mesh gearbox, applied also to 1965 S-types. At the same time the cars were given diaphragm clutches of new design, and a dual-range Borg-Warner automatic box was applied to the big saloons. The 'D1' position on the selector brought all ratios into engagement, but if 'D2' were selected bottom gear was eliminated. This gave a smoother, more leisurely and more frugal get-away. 1965 MkXs also had the latest Marles Varamatic variable-rate power-assisted steering, which gave only three turns from lock to lock and was

universally praised.

During 1965 two new options broadened MkX's appeal further: air conditioning and an electrically-operated division. In 1966, five years after the E-type's sensational debut, it reappeared as a 2+2. Nine inches more wheelbase and two inches of extra body height could not spoil its looks, although top speed dropped to 136mph, and for the first time since 1961 Jaguar's sports-car clientele could opt for automatic if they desired. Even with the added attractions of D1-D2 testers did not altogether approve of these shiftless E-types, but the general concept pleased, Denis Jenkinson of *Motor Sport* confessing that: 'Unless you have just parted from a two-seater E-type coupé you would not know the difference when driving it.' Another 1966 introduction, Bertone of Italy's two-door FT-type sports saloon built up around the mechanical elements of the 3.8-litre S-type, never reached the public.

More variations on a theme, 1967. The 420G was only an up-rated Mk X, but the 420 was a cross between its big sister and the S-type. There was a Daimler version as well

By 1969 the E-type's headlamps had receded behind the 'building line', though other improvements were less immediately noticeable

Partial import duty would have meant a most un-Jaguar-like price of £3,673.

Jaguar joined forces with the British Motor Corporation in the summer of 1966, but as if to remind the world of their continuing independence they had two new models on display at Earls Court that October. This smacked a little of pack-shuffling, especially as the more expensive 420G was in effect a redesignated MkX. The companion 420 was, however, a halfway house between this stately if rapid machine and the S-type, from which it derived most of its mechanical specification. The appointments, front-end styling and engine came from the 420G, though the latter had three carburetters instead of two, and Varamatic, standard on the 420G, was an optional extra on the cheaper version. Variety was now almost limitless, and there were Jaguars to suit every upper-middle-income pocket, from a 2.4-litre MkII at £1,342 to a 2+2 automatic E-type at £2,427. At the same time Daimler enthusiasts noted with regret that the latest Sovereign was only a Jaguar 420 with

a Daimler grille, and this was indicative of future trends. By 1969 both the Majestic Major limousine and British Leyland's other formal carriage, the aged Princess, had been supplanted by a Vanden Plas-bodied eight-seater Daimler using the 4.2-litre Jaguar engine.

The 1967 shows had nothing new to offer, though *Autocar* re-tested a 4.2-litre E-type and found it 'still unique'. Continued their report: 'Its performance, ex-works price, steering, roadholding, tractability, economy, comfort and good looks may be matched by other sports or GT cars, but not one of them has the lot.' A brief sensation was caused by the Piranha, a dream car which Bertone conceived for *Daily Telegraph Magazine* around the E-type's mechanics: complete with 'sawn-off' Kamm-type tail, radio, tape recorder, speed limit 'bleep' warning and an airliner-style 'fasten seat belts' signal, it cost a reputed £20,000 to build. It was subsequently auctioned in New York for a third of this amount.

The big news of 1968, of course, broke in January when BMC-Jaguar fused with the Leyland Group. Shortly afterwards Jaguar told the world that they had spent £250,000 on engineering

their cars to conform with the latest American smoke-emission laws. Increased safety-consciousness was having the same effect on the E-type as racing rules had had on its ancestors. Tests carried out on a standard 2+2 version showed that the model was now 3.2 seconds slower to 100mph, had lost 16mph off its maximum speed, and was 4.2mpg to the bad when cruised at a steady 80mph, a velocity now illegal in Britain as well as in almost every State of the American Union. The overall increase in thirst was, however, only marginal. 1968 E-types for export had key-starting, a hazard warning device in the form of flashers at front and rear, and relocated door and window winders, though the wood-rimmed steering-wheel was retained. Rationalisation was in the air, but Jaguar boasted that they could deliver 189,024 different motor cars without deviating from catalogue specifications. Against an economic background which grew steadily gloomier they could also assert with pride that only twice had they had to produce cars 'just for stock' – during the 1956 Suez Crisis and during a brief period ten years later, at the outset of Harold Wilson's Credit Squeeze.

In his Lord Wakefield Gold Medal Paper on *The Role of the Specialist Car,* delivered in May 1969, Sir William Lyons was to warn his audience that a contender in this field 'must be prepared to change the style and design of his cars more frequently than in the past', and by the time these words were uttered he had done just that, creating yet another show-stopper in the process. The belle of the 1968 Earls Court Show was a new Jaguar saloon, the XJ 6. The 'three-box' unitary construction concentrated its main torsional strength in the centre and below the waistline, with additional stiffness ensured by twin underfloor-mounted cross-members. Gone from the bonnet was the familiar Big Cat; rocker-type switches and a hazard warning system were found inside as well as the traditional wood and leather, and the coil-and-wishbone front suspension had anti-dive properties. Other features were rack-and-pinion steering and Girling servo-assisted disc brakes, a heated rear window was standard, and as an alternative to the 4.2-litre engine buyers could specify a new short-stroke 2.8-litre unit developing 180bhp. Power-assisted steering was standard on the 4.2-litre, and optional on the 2.8. It was noted that the bonnet was 'wide enough to take vee engines', and the knowledgeable hinted that if these came they would not be the old-type Daimlers. Not even growing restrictions could mar the Jaguar style, and by contrast with the MkX the XJ 6 looked less bulky, though not everybody liked the horizontal-barred grille. A 4.2-litre automatic version came up for test during 1969, and was found capable of 120mph in 'high' and 87mph in 'intermediate'. Even if the 'performance image' was no longer stressed, the XJ was as fast overall as the 1957 3.4-litre automatic, and appreciably more accelerative in the lower speed ranges. There was, however, no comparing the ride or handling: the early compacts had always been tricky, but the latest car's neutral steering characteristics were

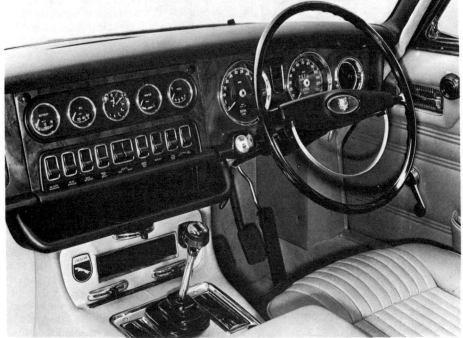

The 1970 XJ 6. Safety regulations have swept away the 'Big Cat' mascot, and a new 'executive' image renders the wire wheels a less common option, but the car is still unmistakably a Jaguar

allied to excellent road-holding qualities, and the car could be cruised at three-figure speeds on French secondary roads without discomfort. The latest Adwest power assisted steering offered positive feel and quick response as well as minimum effort, and *Autocar*'s testers felt that Jaguar could double the existing list price of £2,688 with impunity.

Now that only E-types were going to America, a lot of people hoped that there would, for once, be a quick and steady flow of XJ 6s into dealers' showrooms at home. Quite the reverse happened, so much so, indeed, that nine months after the model's introduction Jaguar ran an advertisement depicting a harassed salesman. 'Don't blame him,' proclaimed the copy, 'blame Jaguar, for building such an enviable reputation. There are always fewer Jaguars than people who want

The 'office' of a manual XJ 6, 1968, marries safety with tradition

them.' (No other manufacturer, of course, could afford the luxury of 'You Can't Have One' publicity when showrooms were full of unsold cars). At the end of the year the factory announced that they had built 28,391 Jaguars and Daimlers, a big improvement on the 1968 total of 23,535, but even in 1971 you cannot walk into a distributor's office with a cheque and emerge a few minutes later at the wheel of an XJ.

A simplified 1970 range consisted of the E-type, the two XJ 6 models and the 420G, the last-mentioned disappearing during the year, as did the open E-type. Daimler's Sovereign became an XJ in all but name, but at the top of British Leyland's vast and complex repertoire of Austins, Morrises, Minis, Wolseleys, MGs, Austin-Healeys, Vanden Plas, Triumphs, Rovers, Jaguars and Daimlers was £5,445-worth of limousine. A lot of money, but less than half the price of a Rolls-Royce. Most of these huge cars were black, and automatic was compulsory, but the bonnet housed a twin-overhead-camshaft six, the legacy of five Le Mans victories.

Surely nobody, gazing on William Lyons' slim bronze roadster for the first time at Earls Court in 1948, could have foreseen this improbable application?

EXPORTS

Ask an American when he first became aware of the Big Cat, and he will probably name a day in the fall of 1949, when some lucky guy rolled into town at the wheel of four thousand bucks' worth of XK 120 roadster. If you tell him that way back in 1934 his father could have procured an SS I Airline fastback sedan in New York City, he will not believe you. If you add that the Jaguar Group have a sixty-five-year record, albeit an interrupted one, of dollar exports, you will be dismissed as a cross between Ananias and Baron

Munchausen.

Britain sold cars in America long before Sir Stafford Cripps offered the choice between mass exports and bankruptcy in 1947. William Lyons was not the first British manufacturer to conduct a sales tour of the United States: the Hon C S Rolls was there on behalf of Rolls-Royce in the autumn of 1906. The inter-war period had even seen two unsuccessful attempts to manufacture British designs on the other side of the Atlantic, and these represented the two extremes – the

40-50hp Rolls-Royce and the Austin Seven. 'The Best Car in The World' failed because Americans imagined (wrongly) that anything made away from Derby must be inferior, and the Austin because they do not really want small cars, however much they ask for them. A baby Austin restyled to look like a Chevrolet was as unacceptable in 1930 as were the original fifteen-footer compacts of the Big Three in 1960.

Exports to America can succeed only where a manufacturer can penetrate a minority market, one which it does not pay Detroit to cultivate. This goes for all the big foreign-car triumphs – MG TCs, the Volkswagen, the Jaguar family, and the small Japanese Toyotas of the 1970s. Make the demand big enough, and Detroit will cope; the Ford Mustang would have been unthinkable in 1954, but ten years later it broke all sales records for any completely new type of car. In the first years of the present century, however, there was a huge gap in the ranks of the native product. Until 1911, America was short on luxury cars in the modern idiom, and while this state of affairs continued, the foreign makers had a field-day. Numbers were small, of course: FIAT considered a single shipment of thirty-one chassis worth a press release in 1908, and the year's best-selling import, Renault, sold a paltry 266 cars. By contrast, Toyota were shipping 7,000 cars a month across the Pacific in 1970, Jaguar have shipped as many as 300 at a time, and when the E-type took its bow in New York in the spring of 1961 six were sold in the first thirty minutes. The foreign-car boom was not killed by the First World War: it was all over by 1913. By this time firms of the calibre of the 'Three Ps' (Packard, Peerless, and Pierce-Arrow) could make luxury carriages comparable with Europe's best, while even in the infant sports-car market Mercer and Stutz had the edge on the big and brutal

British dollar exports in 1934. A line of 1935-model SS Is led by an Airline saloon.

Right-hand drive again in the 1950 Monte Carlo Rally, but the 1948 3½-litre Jaguar drophead coupé was the firm's export-only model

Isotta Fraschinis, Italas and Benz. But it was fun while it lasted, and among the beneficiaries were Daimler. The big chain-driven side-valve fours of the 1904–08 period were excellent performers, and almost unbeatable in hill-climbs. In Britain they dominated club events just as the XKs were to do forty-five years later, and thus there were quite a few buyers for 30-40hp chassis at $6,750 a time, f.o.b. New York. The advent of sleeve-valve engines in 1908 changed the marque's image, of course, and thereafter Daimler's foreign clientele tended to be illustrious and chauffeur-driven. Not even the magnificent 5½-litre straight-eights of the Docker era could make Daimler a major force in the export drive.

As for the Jaguar, its real impact was a post-1945 phenomenon, though an export sale of seven to ten per cent in the later 1930s was not as bad as it sounds. Britain, after all, was no great exporter of cars, and her figure of 20 per cent was closely related to the large areas of red on maps of the world. Patriotism is a strong incentive, and so is Imperial Preference, even if Hillman Minxes and Morris Tens were seldom seen outside the big cities of the Commonwealth, and dwellers in the bush or outback preferred Canadian sedans to their less dust-proof British equivalents. The backbone of Britain's exports to the world outside consisted of what she could make best – luxury cars and inexpensive sporting machinery. The MG was known from the Pacific to the Baltic, and so, by 1939, was William Lyons's SS.

In the 1920s he had adopted the Hayward Universal sidecar chassis, which made left hand drive an easy proposition, and an Austin Swallow saloon was shipped to the Sultan of Perak as early as 1930. Less than 800 of the original 1932-model SS cars were sold, but in recent years examples have been run to ground as far afield as Czechoslovakia, Australia and New Zealand. By 1934 the company had agents in nine European countries as well as in Egypt, Palestine, Morocco, India and Australia, and that autumn the first shipment of 20hp SS Is was on its way to America. Despite the appointment of the Heir to the Spanish Throne as New York salesman, the venture did not prosper, any more than did a second effort by Hilton Motors early in 1936. It is amusing to note that the cars that Hilton advertised were not the latest ohv 2½-litre Jaguars (then selling briskly at home), but SS Is left over from the 1935 season, among them one or two of the seldom-seen drophead coupés.

In Europe, of course, the Jaguar series went down well: SS Cars Ltd published a French-language catalogue in 1938, and the cars were seen at foreign salons – Paris as early as 1936,

and Belgrade in 1939. Swiss coachbuilders fitted Germanic-looking cabriolet bodywork to SS Jaguar chassis, and there were now agencies in Hungary, Yugoslavia and Rumania, where Crown Prince Michael took delivery of one of the first 3½-litre 100 models to be exported.

After the war, of course, Britain found herself a debtor nation. Not only was car production frustrated by every possible kind of shortage, but most of it went abroad, and the whole concept of exports had to be overhauled. No longer could foreign customers be fobbed off with last year's models, a trick played on Britons, incidentally, by American and Continental firms in the 1930s. They could not be expected to make do with what was going, with metric instruments and left-hand drive

Loading the holds of the 'Mauretania' 1949, the reason why Britons seldom got their hands on the Mk V

Hollywood moves in: Clark Gable with his first XK 120, 1950

thrown in if they were lucky. Against the background of a world-wide demand for cars in the 1940s, prompt delivery was what counted, but the wise virgins of Coventry, Paris and Turin were already thinking further ahead. Cars were being designed specifically for world markets, and if some of these were mistakes, like the Austin Atlantic, their makers were at least trying hard. Among those who set their sights higher was William Lyons.

Initially, only twenty-six per cent of Jaguar's production was exported, but the first two peacetime seasons was a three hundred per cent rise in European sales, and this at a time when wholesale petrol rationing hardly favoured cars like the $3\frac{1}{2}$-litre. Belgium, still a colonial power and the first of Hitler's former victims to recover, was particularly fertile soil exploited to the full by the dynamic Mme Bourgeois ('Madame Jaguar'). By mid-1946 she had supplied five $3\frac{1}{2}$-litre saloons for use by Belgian ambassadors abroad, and when a cautious Government clamped down on the import of foreign cars costing over £600, she and Jaguar were ready. For a while six-cylinder models were assembled in the old Vanden Plas coachworks, and the fiscal authorities were hoist with their own petard. Jaguars were now twenty per cent cheaper, so the French specialist manufacturers, who had been making hay with cars they could not sell at home, suddenly felt the pinch.

The Big Cat was also making an impression in Switzerland, if only because Jaguar were the only specialist makers who could deliver the goods. Germany was *hors de combat* and Mercedes-Benz would have nothing new to offer until 1951: BMW and Auto Union, whose main car factories were now in Russian-controlled territory, were no longer even a potential threat. Though Italy's

The first of the many. XK 120s at Foleshill, 1949, en route for the USA

recovery was quicker – FIATs and Lancias were on sale in Switzerland by the end of 1946 – the latter firm's annual output was still below the thousand mark, while the 2½-litre Alfa-Romeo was prohibitively expensive. France, admittedly, had resuscitated her fine pre-war *grand' routiers* – the 3½-litres of Hotchkiss and Delahaye were much in evidence at the 1946 Paris Salon, and the new 4½-litre Talbot was a magnificent car, capable of 115mph. But France was bedevilled with 'Resistance managements', her supply problems were worse than Britain's (high-quality British leather was available only to firms with dollar customers!) and her tax-structure was loaded against anything rated at over 15 chevaux-vapeur – say two-and-three quarter litres. Talbot's racing pro-gramme was more successful than any-one would have expected, but it could not save Talbot. They were in dire trouble by 1952, and though Lago kept going for another six years, the firm eventually closed.

Thus Jaguar was firmly established as an exporter before the advent of either XK 120 or MkVII. Lyons did not tackle America until January 1947, but once his mind was made up, he never let go. Left-hand drive was offered from the start, but the American customer was given what he wanted. Standard bumpers were too fragile, so MkV sprouted heavy protective overriders. American customers pref-erred convertibles; Lyons gave them convertibles. In the summer of 1948 he crossed the Atlantic to see things for himself, signing up agencies and telling the press: 'You cannot get any volume of export business by long-range corres-pondence.' On this, the first of many visits, he went to Hollywood, the heart of the custom-car country, to open a special Jaguar show. Of the sixteen new cars sold, one, a 3½-litre drophead coupé, went to Clark Gable. Mr Gable later bought an XK 120 through Horn-burg, the Southern Californian dis-tributor who is still with Jaguar, twenty-two years later.

The pace, of course, quickened when the XK 120 was announced. The first ninety orders were booked on the strength of the catalogue alone, while at the 1949 European Car Show in New York 200 MkVs found buyers. In October Hoffman Motors, the American distributors, announced that they had reserved the next six months' output of XKs, and the model's American racing debut at Palm Beach in January 1950 was backed at the British Car Exhibition by the sort of display Americans love, a white XK shown on a velvet-covered dais and flanked by Jaguar statuettes in bronze. A further $300,000 worth of Jaguars found buyers as a result. When MkVII came out the following autumn, there was no waiting for the spring shows, either. As soon as the doors closed on Earls Court's last visitor, the metallic-blue prototype was whisked away and displayed in New York's Waldorf-Astoria Hotel, a piece of showmanship which won Jaguar 500 orders from the Eastern States alone. No wonder, for here was

a $3,850 automobile which would do almost anything a Cadillac would do. It became even more attractive in American eyes two years later, when automatic transmission was added to the package. By 1956 automatic was standard on saloons for dollar export. MkVII had penetrated to Australia as early as April 1951, though South Africans could not buy it until the following autumn. A new wood-drying plant was installed at the factory, which cut the time required for this process down to nine minutes, and at the same time immunised the trim against the ravages of the tropics.

The export boom had passed its peak by 1952, when not a few British models could be bought off the showroom floor at home. Not so Jaguars: 84 per cent of 1951's output had gone abroad, but in 1952 Britons got only four per cent! American prices were slashed in 1953, when the four-year-old XK 120 was voted the nation's Sports Car of the Year. Ten years later another relatively old design, the 3.8-litre MkII saloon, was adjudged to be 'the most popular medium-sized car', gaining almost double the number of votes cast for the mass-produced runner-up, Pontiac's Tempest.

The Jaguar credo, of course, extended a long way beyond mere sales. One of the greatest deterrents to ownership of a foreign import is the lack of spares and good service, and it is characteristic of Lyons' approach that the announcement of his new United States sales organisation, Jaguar North American Inc, in 1954 was preceded by an intensive training programme for dealers' staff. By this time it was estimated that 14,000 Jaguars were running on American roads, and nobody was surprised when a new landmark was achieved. Up to now the company had headed the list of foreign imports in terms of dollar value: now they beat even Volkswagen in terms of sheer numbers. A further fillip to the American market was given by the 3.4-litre saloon of 1957, and when the XK 150 roadster was unveiled at the 1958 New York Importers' Show it sold at the rate of one per hour: no wonder this particular model was a rare sight in Britain. At the same time Jaguar North America opened a central spares depot: it was estimated that spares to the value of $60,000 were carried by the average American Jaguar dealer.

As interesting as Jaguar's sales in America was their effect on the native industry. By 1954 both Ford and Chevrolet were trying their luck with sports cars of a sort. The former's Thunderbird did not go on sale until 1955 model year, and was promoted as a 'personal car': a certain individuality of line helped to sell more than 16,000 units in its first season, but despite a top speed of 115-120mph it was not for the enthusiast. Chevrolet's fibreglass-bodied Corvette looked more promising, and beat the Ford to the showrooms by nearly two years: in its original 6-cylinder form, however, it suffered from a regrettable lack of steam. 1954 sales amounted to a disappointing 3,625 units (very close to Jaguar's American total for the year), and confirmed the Jaguar Sales Department's often expressed view that 'to an American, a sports car is an imported car'.

Elsewhere the cars prospered. 700 of the first 1,000 Jaguars delivered after the fire of 1957 went for export, and Mme Bourgeois opened new showrooms in Brussels, the ceremony being attended by the Belgian Premier as well as by Sir William Lyons. That year Nigeria took thirty 2.4-litre saloons, a prelude to the adoption of MkIX as official transport: it was not lost on observers that in pidgin-English the word 'Jagwah' has come to mean 'a man about town'. Late in 1960 an assembly plant in South Africa

started to deliver MkIIs for local consumption, thus circumventing import restrictions which threatened sales in yet another country. (It is interesting to note that Jaguar have avoided Rolls-Royce's American mistake of 1920, and respect the customer's preference for 'fully-imported cars' in the upper echelons of the market. Foreign assembly has only been resorted to when it represented the only means of market-penetration: in South Africa, in Belgium in the 1940s, in Mexico during the 1950s, and in Eire since MkV days).

Despite the Mini and the Ford Cortina the 1960s were not a happy decade for Britain's exporters. Once again, however, Jaguar proved the exception. Perhaps the best illustration of this was Switzerland, a well-to-do country with virtually no native car production, if one excepts the Chrysler-engined exotica of Peter Monteverdi. The early post-war period had seen British penetration at its zenith, with our share of the market rising dramatically from a meagre six per cent in 1939 to nearly thirty-two per cent in 1946-7. Since then, of course, the recovery of the former Axis nations had reversed this situation, and in 1960 West Germany's contribution (45,971 units) formed a depressing comparison with British sales of 7,674. Even Italy, which in effect, meant FIAT, had sold 8,240 cars in Switzerland. But while the Big Battalions faded out of the picture, Jaguar's share went up, from 296 cars in 1959 to 476 in 1960. Their 1964 sales of 465 units sound poor beside the efforts of Mercedes-Benz (3,050) and Rover (1,160), but the German concern relied heavily on their bread-and-butter 190D diesel, which was popular as a taxi, while Rover's figures included the ubiquitous Land-Rover, a 'specialist car' of a totally different kind. As matters stood, Jaguar had outsold Porsche, and their prices remained competitive. The 2.4-litre cost only £50 more than the comparable Mercedes, and in the sports-car sector the E-type continued to undercut the

opposition.

Britain's continued exclusion from the Common Market rendered France a far more difficult market to penetrate, the French tax-structure still limiting the sales potential of the bigger cars, anyway. A Frenchman had good reason for preferring a Mercedes saloon to the comparable compact Jaguar; – buying German saved him a cool £350. But in spite of this Jaguar's French sales rose by fifty-three per cent in 1963 – well above the Western European average of forty per cent. The E-type at £2,739 was fractionally cheaper than the 230SL Mercedes-Benz, and if £2,883 was a lot of money for the MkX, it was a better buy than £4,300-worth of Cadillac.

Another promising market was West Germany. Thanks to the racing successes of Jaguar's concessionaire, Peter Lindner, a bridgehead was established in Mercedes-Benz' home territory. There was, of course, no hope of direct competition with Stuttgart's cheaper sixes, which sold at around the £1,000 mark, less than half the price of a MkII. A wide gap also separated the Mk X from the comparable 300SE saloon, while a differential of DM7,100 gave the E-type less chance

The C–type at the 1953 Brussels Salon. It wore Belgium's national yellow with considerable success

against its familiar rival, the 230SL roadster. Nevertheless, by July 1964 the *Bundesrepublik* registered 1,150 Jaguars; a drop in the ocean beside the country's 550,000 Mercedes and 15,000 Porsches, but a creditable performance in a land which led Europe in car production. What is more, Jaguar were in Germany to stay, and by 1968 they were tailoring their models to German requirements. 420s destined for Lindners' conformed both to law and to local tastes. The former demanded laminated screens, twin wing mirrors, and no Big Cat: the latter expressed itself in terms of 3.31 back axles, automatic gearboxes, power-assisted steering, heated rear windows, and wire wheels (from which officialdom deleted the eared hubs).

The same picture was reflected elsewhere. 1964 saw significant improvement in Danish and Swedish sales, and even Italy, traditionally a closed shop, was slowly opening its doors to foreign marques. At £2,110 the MkII Jaguar was cheaper than a Mer-

137

cedes-Benz, and it offered more than any of the native opposition, even if a Lancia Flaminia cost only £1,687, and FIAT 2300S with 2+2 bodywork was a bargain at £1,552. Belgians took kindly to MkII, which in 2.4-litre form could be bought for less than £1,500 in 1967, and eventually undercut Mercedes-Benz before it was withdrawn in 1969. In the first seven months of that year, Jaguar's South African assemblers established a new record by turning out 1,078 cars.

Jaguar had every reason to feel proud of their achievements. An advertisement published in March 1968 spelled these out in bold type. The firm had earned £56 million in export markets over a period of four years, they were exporting nearly fifty-two per cent of their overall output, and ninety-five per cent of their E-types, and still there were not enough of these latter to satisfy America. Jaguars sold through a network of 134 distributors and 960 dealers in 126 countries.

All this, of course, demanded a high degree of organisation. A forecast of the ratio of home to export sales was made twelve months ahead of schedule. Foreign distributors then fed their model-by-model breakdowns back to Coventry, but even then it was not just a matter of making cars and loading them aboard ship. Other factors must be considered, such as the legal requirements of certain countries, and the thousand-odd cars annually earmarked for 'personal export'. These were handled in Britain, and were given priority. Even the actual shipment had its problems. Certain items, such as the transistorised clocks, were eminently pilferable, and could land the company in claims of up to $70 per car. Such losses could be circumvented by using individual containers for each car (a method applied during 1969 in the case of vehicles destined for Australia), but this raised the shipping cost; therefore on the American run the items were packed separately. There were still not enough Jaguars to go round. America might no longer be taking saloons, but a letter to *Autocar* as late as February 1971 observed that Australians were faced with an eighteen months' wait for a new XJ6. 'They did not really believe me,' the writer concluded, 'on being told that the British market had to wait as long.'

As for America, the picture changed little. Overall speed limits had no effect on E-type sales, especially after a $300 price cut in 1963. A year later Detroit had another stab at making a sporting car.

Ford's Mustang, unlike its predecessors, was an instant success, to the tune of half a million cars in its first eighteen months. Unlike the Jaguar, it was a full four-seater, and with the optional 4.7-litre V8 engine it was capable of 116mph. It was also compact by American standards, with a length of 15ft 2in, and by 1965 it had made its mark in European rallies and saloon-car races, even if Europeans looked upon it as a prestige-machine rather than as a sporty means of transportation. It was also what its sponsors termed a 'personalised automobile', with two pages of options occupying the back of the catalogue. In 1968 buyers had the choice of twelve 'power teams', from a 115bhp straight-six up to a 7-litre V8 disposing of 390bhp, allied to 3- and 4-speed manual gearboxes and the usual American automatics. Hot on the heels of the Mustang came its imitators: Lincoln-Mercury Division's Cougar, Chevrolet's Camaro, and Dodge's Charger.

In stock form, the Mustang was tricky in the wet, and the fiercer 8-cylinder engines were both finicky and thirsty. It did, however, offer Americans something new and individual, and at a bargain price. The regular Mustang V8 hardtop retailed for $2,822 in 1970, compared with the $5,725 asked for an E-type. Sir William Lyons struck a warning note when he described the Mustang and its rivals as 'the modern equivalent of the specialist car of earlier days'. 'They may not,' he continued, 'represent a thoroughbred version of the specialist car, but they do provide cars which are different, and which

offer a particular type of motoring.'
In 1971, incidentally, Ford considered it
worth while to challenge the smaller
imported machinery with their Pinto,
using German or British-built Ford
engines.

For all Sir William's warnings, the
4.2-litre E-type continued to provide
an adequate answer, and Jaguar were
doing a lot better in America than were
their new partners, the British Motor
Corporation. On a weekly output of
500-600 units they were earning £7
million a year from American sales.
BMC's annual dollar income was triple
this amount: but then they were making
20,000 cars a week. Further, their share
of the market was declining. Com-
parative statistics for 1959 and 1967
made depressing reading for most
British manufacturers. BMC, who had
shipped 68,762 cars in the former year,
were down eight years later to 32,726,
a drop of over fifty per cent. Others,
notably Ford of Dagenham and the
Rootes Group, fared appreciably
worse. Jaguar recorded only a drop of
three per cent: less than anyone except
Rover, who had actually strengthened
their position in the United States: not
that the comparison was fair, for in 1959
the Solihull firm had nothing calculated
to appeal to an American, whereas
since 1964 they had offered the 2000,
a saloon of some performance with
built-in safety features. As this retailed
for $3,088, well below the cheapest
Jaguar on the United States market, one

Selling in a free market: E-type and S-type saloon at Geneva, 1964

would have expected the marque to
outsell the Big Cat. But it did not: in 1967
Americans bought 5,733 Jaguars, but
only 2,703 Rovers.

If BMC benefited from the alliance
with Jaguar, the fusion of interests led to
better export coverage, not only in
America where a central parts depot at
Leonia, New Jersey, claimed to offer
ninety-nine per cent of dealers' possible requirements on a 24-hour basis,
but also in Switzerland, where a new
firm, British Leyland AG, was formed to
distribute not only BMC and Jaguar
products but also the Rover and
Triumph products now gathered under
the same banner.

By 1969 the safety and smoke-emission rules had thinned the ranks of
American imports: even the well-loved
Morgan was no longer quoted in the
United States. But Jaguar, which now
meant the E-type alone, went marching
on. It cost £250,000 to make the model
legal, and in the process it lost a
modicum of both looks and performance. The engine was de-rated to
give 245bhp, while other changes included a 'federalised' facia, exposed
headlamps, a collapsible steering-
column and a full-width front bumper. It
was worth it, though; the first six
months of 1970 set a new record for
Jaguar in America, with 3,536 cars sold.

MERGERS

The announcement that appeared in the daily papers on the morning of 12th July 1966 took Britain by storm. Jaguar, the Great Independent, was to merge with the British Motor Corporation.

Somehow it hurt. 'Merger' was synonymous with 'take-over' in most people's minds, and in the motor industry a take-over meant one of two things; a slow rundown or a dose of badge-engineering. Rootes had acquired Clement Talbot Ltd in 1935; three years later the last traces of Georges Roesch's inspired engineering had gone. In America, the Studebaker and Packard interests had merged in 1954, but the 1957 Packards turned out to be only expensive Studebakers, and by 1959 there were no Packards at all: not that it saved Studebaker, who had taken Canadian nationality in 1964, and expired quietly a few months before the conclusion of the BMC-Jaguar deal. In France the ancient house of Panhard-Levassor was breathing its last as a Citroën subsidiary.

Only six years previously, people recalled, Jaguar had suddenly become an empire in its own right. The purveyors of non-standard Standards had come a long way since 1932, and the purchase of Daimler by Sir William Lyons in 1960 had saved a great name from creeping paralysis. It had also given Jaguar a foothold in hitherto unexplored territory – the omnibus.

Alongside their cars, Daimler had been building buses since 1908, and for a brief period (1926-29) they had joined forces on the commercial-vehicle side with AEC of London. With independence once more came the restoration of the fluted radiator to Daimler buses, and in 1930 the fluid-flywheel transmission was introduced. Diesels, initially Gardners, but later of Daimler design and manufacture appeared on the scene in 1933, a semi-

The Daimler heritage: Lord Montagu drives the legendary 1899 4-cylinder Paris-Ostend car, once his father's property, in the 1970 London-Brighton Run

automatic 'Daimatic' gearbox in 1957, and a modern layout with transverse, rear-mounted engine in 1960. In the 1960s more than half Britain's municipal operators used Daimlers; among these were Aberdeen, Birmingham, Bournemouth, Bradford, Cardiff, Chester, Derby, Edinburgh, Glasgow, Halifax, Huddersfield, Leeds, Leicester, Liverpool, Manchester, Northampton, Nottingham, Portsmouth, Sheffield, Southend, Sunderland, Walsall, West Hartlepool and Wolverhampton. Other Daimler customers included London Transport, Midland Red, Potteries Motor Traction, and Yorkshire Woollen District, while by 1966 Daimlers were in service in seventeen Commonwealth and foreign countries. Shortly after the take-over production was re-organised. Daimler's car side was transferred to Browns Lane, leaving the assembly halls at Radford clear to cope with buses.

The next step came in November 1961, when Guy Motors of Wolverhampton were added to the fold.

If Daimler had always kept a foot in the heavy camp, trucks had been Guy's predominant interest since the beginning in 1914. Their private cars had a brief life (1919-25) and are memorable mainly because they included Britain's first series-production vee-eight. But during their long career Guy had explored every aspect of truck manufacture; their cross-country vehicles had included 4×4 designs for the War Office as early as 1938, gas-producer lorries in 1927, and even battery-electrics. Like Daimler, they had also done well out of buses, being responsible for Britain's first six-wheeled double-decker in 1926. During the Second World War they had turned out hundreds of the famous 'austerity' Arabs with slatted wooden seats, which replaced public-service vehicles written off by enemy action, and after the Sunbeam debacle of 1935 they acquired that firm's trolleybus interests. (At the time when Jaguar moved in, they were still making trolleybuses, mainly for export.) Guy were the bespoke makers

141

Best of the Daimler range at the time of the Jaguar purchase, the Vee-eight Majestic Major saloon. This one was owned by the late Lord Brabazon of Tara

par excellence: they asserted that they could produce anything the customer wanted, and in the end this road led to receivership. Their 1961 range embraced everything from the modest 4-ton Vixen with 58bhp diesel engine up to eight-wheeler versions of the huge Invincible capable of carrying 24-ton payloads, while a variety of bus types included the advanced, air-sprung Wulfrunian double-decker. Jaguar's first task at 'The Motors', as the Guy factory in Wolverhampton was known locally, was to rationalise the programme. Nevertheless, however run-down Guy might be, a survey published at the end of 1961 showed that no fewer than 5,762 of the 17,390 municipally-operated omnibuses in Britain were of 'Jaguar' manufacture, made up of course of Daimlers and Guys.

In March 1963, Coventry Climax Engines Ltd joined the Jaguar empire. This, according to Jaguar's own publication, *Case History*, 'brought together two of the finest teams of engineers in the industry', for the newest acquisition, though in its younger years renowned as a supplier of proprietary engines (among the better-known clients had been Clyno, Crossley, Morgan and Triumph) had enjoyed two vastly different, but equally distinguished reputations since 1939. Britain's Civil Defence in the Second World War had leaned heavily on Coventry-Climax trailer fire pumps, powered, incidentally, by leftover engines intended for the abortive 8hp Swift of 1931. The year 1950, however, had seen the first of the FW series of overhead-camshaft 4-cylinder units, built to a Government fire-pump specification. These had evolved into a brilliant series of single- and twin-cam racing engines, which played a vital part in Britain's Formula I rennaissance. Coventry-Climax gave Jack Brabham his two

142

World Championships in 1959 and 1960; they performed the same service for the late Jim Clark in 1963 and 1965; they powered Colin Chapman's first 'civilized' motor car, the Lotus Elite coupé; and the 875cc Hillman Imp unit, announced less than two months after its creator had changed hands, was also based on a Coventry-Climax idea. The last year of the 1,500cc Formula saw a new and ingenious flat-sixteen, but Jaguar were quick to make it clear that this was to be the last racing engine. Instead, they concentrated on two safe bread-and-butter lines: the fire pumps and a range of fork-lift trucks (Britain's first, incidentally) which had been making many friends since 1946. As early as 1951 Coventry-Climax had also pioneered the use of diesel engines in small industrial vehicles of this type.

The empire was rounded out a couple of years later by the addition of Coventry-Climax's erstwhile rivals in the proprietary engine field, Henry Meadows of Wolverhampton. While the Coventry-Climax F-head motors of the 1930s had been largely ordinary units, Meadows had latterly catered for a more sporting market with their push-rod ohv types, of which the best-known were the $1\frac{1}{2}$-litre 4ED used by Lea-Francis and Frazer Nash, and the big 4,467cc four-bearing six developed for Invicta in 1928, and taken up to such good purpose six years later by Lagonda. This tough engine was also adapted for marine use, and was fitted to a number of British light tanks. The last Meadows design to see service in a private car was the twin-cam 3-litre made for the elaborate and unsaleable Invicta Black Prince in 1946, but since then the company had done well with marine diesels, marine gearboxes (Sir Francis Chichester's Gipsy Moth IV had a Meadows-TMP installation), and large oil engines for trucks and railcars. Already Guy were among their customers, and as the two factories adjoined each other, the role of Meadows was easy to determine. They were put to work assembling engine-gearbox units for the new Big J range being built 'over the fence'.

These new Guy trucks represented the principal innovation of Jaguar's short career as a manufacturer of heavy lorries. They featured forward control and modern all-steel cabs with excellent all-round vision, and were available in four-, six- and eight-wheeler versions with a diversity of diesel engines. The standard unit was the American 9.6-litre vee-six Cummins, but the bigger 12,170cc Cummins NH-220 and the $10\frac{1}{2}$-litre in-line Gardner were also used, as was (at a later date) Perkins' 8.4-litre Model-510 vee-eight. In 1966 Meadows took up the manufacture of the Cummins range. The integration of Guy and Daimler had one further effect: Guy buses disappeared in 1968.

Curiously enough the creation of British Motor Holdings, as the BMC-Jaguar empire was now known, though it brought together nine makes of private car and four makes of truck or bus, resulted in a negligible amount of model-overlap. The makes which died were no longer relevant, for Riley had been on their way out since the Rose-designed twin-camshaft engine was superseded in 1957, and the parallel ranges of Austin and Morris-Commercial trucks were a shameless case of badge-engineering. Neither Daimler nor Jaguar built a small car, while the commercials of the Austin-Morris group offered nothing weightier than a 7/8-tonner. The only possible clash lay between the formal Daimlers and the two 4-litre Vanden Plas Princess models, neither of them significant sellers.

Nonetheless, the new combine could claim an impressive degree of market-penetration: forty-four per cent of home sales. It was made clear that Jaguar would continue under Lyons' chairmanship, with 'the greatest possible degree of autonomy'. But enthusiasts pondered sadly over the Riley's decline. They also looked nearer home at the gradual disappearance of the Daimler. 'Distinctively Different – It's A Daimler', had been Radford's slogan in the 1940s: but under Jaguar control the SP250

**Lightweight Guy. The successful
30cwt model of 1922**

was dropped before the close of 1964,
and so far the only entirely new model
from Daimler had been the 2½-litre
vee-eight saloon, a 2.4-litre MkII Jaguar
with a different engine. The Majestic
Major, last of the 'real' Daimlers, was
to disappear during 1968, and within
eighteen months Edward Turner's
excellent 8-cylinder power unit was
to go as well. What had happened
to Daimler and Riley and to MG could
happen to Jaguar once BMC had laid
hands on them.

Initially little happened, apart from
some much needed tidying-up of
foreign representation: but scarcely
had the public digested all this than
British Motor Holdings themselves merged with the Leyland Group to form the
British Leyland Motor Corporation in
January 1968. This was something of a
surprise, in spite of BMC's recent
unhappy labour-relations record. It was

also a case of 'Britons, Stand Together'.
Already the Nuffield-Austin amal-
gamation of 1951 had reduced Britain's
Big Six to a Big Five, and of these five
only two were all-British. Ford had
always been American-owned, of
course, Vauxhall had made the Big
League solely on the strength of
absorption by General Motors in 1925,
and the financial troubles of the Rootes
Group had been alleviated (if not
cured) by the Chrysler take-over of
1964. Now that all the American giants
had a stake in Britain's industry, it was
time for an alliance between BMC-
Jaguar and Leyland. This famous
heavy-vehicle maker, already a sizeable empire in its own right, had
entered the private-car sector by
buying Standard-Triumph, weakest of
the original Big Six, in 1959, and fol-

**Jaguar-built commercial. The 'Big
J' range of Guys appeared after the
Jaguar take-over and restored the
once-ailing company**

lowing this with the purchase of Rover, and therefore Alvis, in 1966.

If the massed ranks of 1966 had been alarming, those of 1968 verged on the monopolistic: in fact it was now easier to count the 'outsiders' in the car and truck industries. On the car side the newcomers were of course Rover and Triumph, plus the former's four-wheel-drive range which had a foot in both camps. The goods-vehicle line-up was far more complex, including as it did the parent Leyland company, its subsidiaries Albion of Glasgow and Scammell of Watford, plus AEC (Southall) and Thornycroft (Basingstoke), this last now confined to off-the-road machinery such as oilfield tractors and airport crash tenders. Also exclusively a truck-maker was Alvis, whose splendid 3-litre had died of rationalisation in 1967. In the 'heavy' field the independents were Atkinson, Dennis, ERF, Foden and Seddon, all relatively small: while the biggest surviving independent car-maker was, incredibly Reliant of Tamworth, who had started in

HBF 574H

a modest way with three-wheelers, adding a range of sports four-wheeler models in 1961. Certainly the new-born colossus could command a work-force of 200,000 and potential yearly sales worth £800 million. According to *Autocar* it marketed forty different private-car models, though when the permutations of the badge-engineer were forgotten this boiled down to something like twenty-three 'shapes'

The mainstay of Guy production in the 'thirties was building trolley-buses, now an obsolete mode of transport in Britain

The largest single order ever received by Daimler came from London Transport in 1969. 1975 one–man–operated 'Fleetlines' are currently in process of being delivered

and sixteen basic engines. This was certainly an indigestible meal for any corporation, especially in the middle of a credit squeeze.

Sir Donald Stokes, BLMC's boss, started to weed almost immediately, jettisoning the two big Vanden Plas models, but nothing terrible happened at Browns Lane. A certain amount of

A 1937 4½-litre Daimler straight-8 takes George VI to receive the keys of Edinburgh Castle

alarm was felt during 1969, when some drastic regrouping took place: 'popular' offerings, which included the MG and the Austin-Healey, were lumpéd together into the Austin-Morris Division, Jaguar's commercial-vehicle interests passed into the hands of the Truck and Bus Division, and Jaguar-Daimler joined Rover and Triumph in a new Specialist Car Division. The humble and ageing Triumph Herald and the E-type Jaguar were the strangest of bedfellows, but in October came a reassuring statement from Mr A C Swindle, Triumph's General Manager. He told reporters: 'It is not the intention to produce a Triumph with a Rover badge or a Rover with a Jaguar badge, or any other similar permutation. We shall continue to foster a competitive spirit.'

Was all this necessary? Could not Jaguar have remained independent? Gloomy prophets have foretold a Western Europe in which the industry consists of the American satellites, Daimler-Benz/Volkswagen, British Ley-land, and FIAT, plus such state-owned concerns as Alfa-Romeo and Renault, which the big capitalist empires cannot touch. FIAT, certainly ,are going places, with Lancia, Ferrari and Citroën-Maserati in tow. Even Japan, still a young country by the standards of the International Big League, is moving steadily in the direction of a Big Two (Nissan and Toyota). Nissan have already digested Prince Motors and have a stake in Fuji Heavy Industries (Subaru). Toyota's dominions include Daihatsu and Hino, the latter's private cars disappearing as a consequence.

An obstinate independence can maintain a tradition, but it can also lead to impecunious atrophy, especially against a background of spiralling tooling costs. As Sir William Lyons himself has pointed out, specialist makers need to change their designs more frequently, if only to hold off the challenge of Detroit's new generation of 'personalised automobiles'. A re-fusal to accept this axiom would condemn still more firms to the fate of

Still a Daimler, but with body by
Vanden Plas, and twin-cam 4.2-litre
engine by Jaguar: the 1968
limousine

tion – after Lyons, who?

A further awful warning to the
devotees of independence for independence's sake came in February 1971
with the collapse of Rolls-Royce. The
cars were not to blame, for at the time
of bankruptcy they were actually
showing a profit, but the lesson was
clear, in the reddest of red ink. Even
the 'safest' of outside interests, in the
shape of vast government contracts,
was no insurance against a squeeze.
While nobody would willingly have
seen Rolls-Royce as a division of any
other company, such an affiliation
would have assured the continuance of
'the best car in the world'.

Mr Swindle's promise was kept.
Though 1971 saw the faithful six enter
upon its twenty-third season with the
XJ's wide bonnet still unfilled to
capacity, there were stirrings at Allesley, where a new design team, Walter
Hassan and Harry Mundy, had lately
assumed the mantle of Heynes and
Baily, now enjoying a well-earned
retirement. Not that Hassan was new to
Jaguar: he had first joined the firm back
in 1938, and had played a part in the
original XK programme before moving
on to a distinguished career with
Coventry-Climax.

At the end of March the long-
awaited V-12 took its bow. Some people
were disappointed to see it applied
neither to the XJ 6 nor to a mid-engined
E-type replacement, especially after
Sir William Lyons' observations in his
1969 lecture. The new Series 3 E-type
was, however, a tribute to the ageless-
ness of the 1961 shape, not to mention
the classic 4.2-litre 6-cylinder unit,
which was continued as a low-cost
option.

Beneath the traditional outline, however, lay many changes. The car was
nine inches longer, making for wider
doors and greater luggage capacity,
and a wider track made for still better

the old Sunbeam company, who strug-
gled on with a line of beautifully-
engineered carriages until the bitter
end in 1935. The preface to their
penultimate catalogue was entitled 'The
Making of a Vintage Car': one suspects
that the irony was unconscious, but the
main beneficiaries of those last few
hundred Twenties and Twenty-Fives
were neither management, workers
nor shareholders, but the Vintage
enthusiasts of our own generation!

In any case, even a firm of the calibre
of Jaguar, making around 30,000 units a
year, is still dependent on outside firms
for many a component, and such suppliers are often controlled by the
Big Battalions. Jaguar, for instance,
bought their saloon hulls from Pressed
Steel of Oxford, a BMC subsidiary. Thus
a sudden slump in BMC's presswork
orders could have had an adverse
effect on what Jaguar had to pay: and
inevitably the cost would be passed on
to the customer. It is also well to remember that Jaguar has always been a
family concern, which poses the ques-

The 'gasworks': an underbonnet view of the 1971 V-12 unit in the Series 3 E-type. The superb finish is still evident

handling. The turning circle was reduced, and other differences embraced a stiffer front sub-frame to take the new power unit, anti-dive front suspension geometry, improvements to the servo-assisted disc brakes, and ventilated disc wheels with wide rims. Closed bodies had through-flow ventilation, and the wooden steering-wheel rim had given way to one in alloy, leather-covered: the column, of course, was collapsible. The two-seater coupé was no longer offered, but enthusiasts noted with pleasure that along with the 2+2, a roadster was reinstated in the catalogue. The rumoured five-speed gearbox did not materialise, but all E-types could now be had with automatic transmissions.

The big news was, of course, the engine, a 5.3-litre, 60-degree V-12 of oversquare (90×70mm) dimensions, developing 314bhp. This configuration was dictated in part by the need for smoothness and flexibility, but at the same time there was a sidelong glance at the snob-appeal of multi-cylinderism. The Aston Martin, Bentley and Maserati were now eights, and since the war the only twelves on the open market had been the two Italian exotics, Ferrari and Lamborghini, both of them produced in small numbers (total production of both factories in 1968 amounted to less than 1,200 units, whereas during the first nine months of 1970 alone the British market, never a priority customer, had registered 1,141 new E-types). Now Jaguar were offering the benefits of twelve cylinders to a far wider clientele.

They were not, of course, pioneers of quantity-produced V-12s. As far back as 1932 America's 12-cylinder Auburn had been catalogued at under $1,000, though this was very much a 'stripped figure' and $1,250 would be a more realistic idea of the delivered price. This one had made little impact, but the same could not be said of Ford's Lincoln-Zephyr, a middle-class sedan which survived for a dozen years, and sold 15,000-20,000 a season. It was, however, anything but sporting in character, and an engine life of 15,000 miles between overhauls explains why it was thankfully jettisoned by the new management at Dearborn in 1948. In any case, it was made as a V-12 rather than as a V-8 because the Lincoln image of the day, dictated by the costly and superbly-engineered Model-K, demanded the presence of the four extra cylinders.

Jaguar had been 'thinking on twelve' since racing days, and had tested a prototype 5-litre four ohc unit with fuel injection from which 500bhp had been extracted at 8,000rpm. For production

Traditional cockpit layout on the 12-cylinder E-type. It was planned to be left-hand steering all the way, to keep pace with American demands

purposes the original top-end layout had been discarded in favour of a single overhead camshaft per block because a two-stage chain drive would have been too complex. Fuel injection, though not ruled out of court even in 1971, was shelved since a conventional four-carburetter set-up was more easily adapted to smoke-emission techniques: for the toughest export markets – Sweden, the United States and Canada – Series 3 E-types were fitted with crankshaft-driven air pumps to reduce emission levels by oxidising the un-burnt exhaust gases. The most interest-ing feature of the new engine was its Lucas Opus transistorised ignition, which requires no maintenance and offers consistent timing during the unit's life-span. Unlike the six, the twelve had an alloy block which saved some 116 lbs, and brought the end-

product out only 80 lbs heavier than the existing engine. The chassis of the 6- and 12-cylinder E-types were identi-cal, sharing the same new cross-hatched radiator grille, but the bigger version was distinguishable by its four tailpipes. Power-assisted steering was optional with the 4.2-litre engine, but standard on 5.3-litre models.

Performance figures taken on a standard home-market coupé showed little material difference from those achieved by the weekly press on 1965 versions of the 4.2-litre: a maximum speed of 150mph, and 0-100mph ac-celeration time of 16.15 seconds, and a standing quarter-mile in 14.5 seconds. But older motorists who recalled Britain's last sporting 12-cylinder car, W O Bentley's 1938 Lagonda 4½-litre, were aware that the effortless flow of power conferred by the extra

bank of 'pots' would reinstate Jaguar in the Big League. It was 1949, or 1961, all over again.

If the new model's prices seemed less sensational than of old, this was the fault of inflation, not Jaguar. In 1971 it was possible to spend over £1,000 on a British Leyland Mini without deviating one iota from catalogue specification: therefore if in 1949 an XK 120 cost £1,275 as against £360 for a Morris Minor, then £3,500 was about par for a V-12 twenty-two years later. In fact a roadster with manual transmission cost only £3,123, and £256 was saved if the 6-cylinder engine were specified. The result was more than competitive with such offerings as the 280SL Mercedes-Benz (£4,473) and the DB6 Aston Martin (£5,501). As for Ferrari and Lamborghini, they belonged to a different world: Maranello's 365GTC

A Series 3 E-type hardtop showing the new grille with its XJ overtones: count the tailpipes to identify the Twelve from the Six

was expensive enough at £7,901, but the simplest Lamborghini a Briton could buy, the front-engined Jarama, listed at a resounding £9,800. This meant $20,000 plus to Americans, of course.

In their press release Jaguar added that their latest power unit 'will be offered as an alternative . . . for the much sought-after XJ saloon', though they declined to name a day for his happy event. In the summer of 1972 the marriage was consummated; a nice touch was to assign the Double Six name to the Daimler variant, as a tribute to Europes's first series-production twelve-cylinder model introduced in 1926.

The Series 3 E-type in roadster and
2 + 2 coupé versions

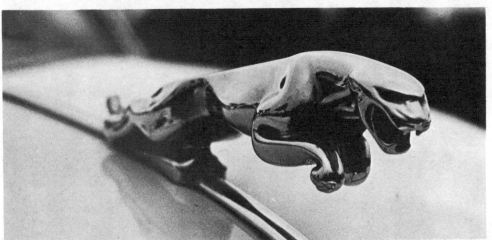

The Author
Lord Montagu of Beaulieu

Edward Montagu, Third Baron of
Beaulieu, was educated at Ridley
College, Canada, Eton and
Oxford. He is one of the world's
foremost motoring personalities,
having written several books on
motoring matters, including a
standard work of reference on
Jaguar in 1961. Lord Montagu is
perhaps best known for his
efforts in establishing the
Montagu Motor Museum within
the grounds of his ancestral
home in Hampshire, England.

Film production Piagraph Limited
Ballantine Consultant Editor Prince Marshall
Foulis Production Editor Tim Parker